1001 Ways to Make More Money as a Speaker, Consultant, or Trainer

Plus 300 Rainmaking Strategies for Dry Times

Lilly Walters

McGraw-Hill

New York   Chicago   San Francisco   Lisbon   London
Madrid   Mexico City   Milan   New Delhi
San Juan   Seoul   Singapore
Sydney   Toronto

The **McGraw·Hill** Companies

1 2 3 4 5 6 7 8 9 0 AGM/AGM 0 9 8 7 6 5 4 3

This publication is designed to provide accurate and authoritative information in regard to the subject matter covered. It is sold with the understanding that neither the author nor the publisher is engaged in rendering legal, accounting, or other professional service. If legal advice or other expert assistance is required, the services of a competent professional person should be sought.

—From a declaration of principles jointly adopted by a committee of the American Bar Association and a committee of publishers.

 This book is printed on recycled, acid-free paper containing a minimum of 50% recycled de-inked fiber.

McGraw-Hill books are available at special quantity discounts to use as premiums and sales promotions, or for use in corporate training programs. For more information, please write to the Director of Special Sales, Professional Publishing, McGraw-Hill, Two Penn Plaza, New York, NY 10121-2298. Or contact your local bookstore.

Walters, Lillet.
    1001 ways to make more money as a speaker, consultant, or trainer : plus 300 rainmaking strategies for dry times / by Lilly Walters.
        p. cm.
    Includes index.
    ISBN 0-07-142802-X (alk. paper)
    1. Business consultants—Fees.   2. Motivational speakers—Fees.   3. Employee training personnel—Fees.   4. Advertising.   5. Marketing.   6. Income.   I. Title: One thousand one ways to make more money as a speaker, consultant, or trainer.
II. Title.
HD69.C6W355 2003
001'.068—dc21

2003013300

To Daddy, who filled my life with love.

Contents

Introduction   ix

1. Income Streams   1

Income Sources for Speakers, Trainers, or Consultants   1
    Let Us Count the Ways Experts Generate Income   1
    Authoring and Other Products   2
    Public Seminars   3
    Expert Witness Reports   3
    Infomercial Host   3
    Commercials   3
    Keynote Speeches   3
    Breakouts and Concurrent Sessions   4
    Master of Ceremonies   4
    Panel Moderator   5
    Panel Coordinator and Creator   5
    Panel Participant   5
    Game Show Host for Meeting Events   5
    Partner (Spouse) Programs   6
    Youth Programs   6
    Pre or Post Programs   7
    Pre or Post Locale Tours   7
    Local Historical Characters   7
    Entertainment   7
    Add-on Event Ideas: Pictures   7
    Training   8
    In-House Seminars and Workshops   8
    Moderator or Facilitator   9
    Consultant   9

Work for a Consulting Firm   10
One-on-One Executive Trainer   10
Coach   10
Conference Calls   11
Creating a Hotline Service   12
After-Hours Tutor   12
Company Training Films and Videos   12
Sponsors   12
Spokesperson   13
Seminars to Promote a Client   14

Hire Yourself: Public Seminars and Events   14
Filling the Seats   15
Phone Seminars   16
Working with Public Seminar Producers   16
Share the Gate   17
Adventures, Seminars at Sea, and Resorts   19
Continuing Education Marketplace   19
Virtual Seminars: Correspondence School to Net
    Classrooms   20

Free Speaking: Profiting from Nonfee Presentations   21
Benefits of Nonfee Presentations   22
Ways to Find Paying Customers in Your Nonfee Talks   23
Service Clubs   23
More Ways to Give It Away—And Profit!   24

2. Those Who Buy and Why   25

Where, Why, and How Buyers Will Buy You   25
Where Do You Find Buyers?   25
How to Penetrate Large Companies   29
Why Buyers Like, Buy, and Dislike You   32

Agents, Speakers' Bureaus, and Middlemen   32
Bureaus Dislike You Because . . .   33
You Annoy Bureaus When You Call Because . . .   36
Brokers Are Impressed When You Try to "Sell" Them
    Because . . .   37
Stand out in the Crowd With Speakers' Bureaus   40

3. Rainmaking to Fill Your Income Streams   42

What You Need to Know   42
Don't Quit Your Day Job   42
Get Back to Basics   42

Associate with and Study Successful Experts in Your Industry   44
Hire a Coach or Mentor   44
What Makes the Greatest Presenters?   45

The Basics of Rainmaking   47
The Expert and Leading Authority: The Highest Paid of All!   47
Search in Every Niche and Cranny   48
Become a Celebrity in a Small Pond: Branding   49
Does Anyone Like You? Sidelong Looks   50
Ways that Work While You're Out Working   51
More and More Income-Increasing Tips and Strategies   54
Just Smart Business   57

Promotional Strategies   58
Raving Fan Relationships: One-on-One Marketing   59
Ways to Keep Your Name Current   62
Promotional Systems and Ideas   64

Cultivating Sales, Repeats, Spins-offs, and Referrals   68
Getting Booked a Second Time   68
Ask for Referrals   68
Creating New Engagements from the Present One   69
Rewards and Gifts for Referrers   73
Marketing Strategies for Keeping in Touch   73
Sharing and Networking to Gain Referrals   74
Sales and Negotiating Skills   78

Becoming Famous: Articles, Newsletters, Magazines,
and the Press   84
Where to Find Media Contacts   84
Get the Media to Use Your Material   86
How to Get the Press to Notice You   87
Publicity Releases that Get Results   90
Get Your Articles out into the World   92
When They Say No   95

Road Warriors: Brainy Business and Balance   95
Schedules: Are You Available?   96
What To Do if You're Already Booked   98
Miscellaneous Ideas to Create Income While on the Road   99
Alternatives to the Traditional Office Staff   102
Balancing Your Career and Family   105
Procrastination and Organization   106
Time Savers   107

4. Double Your Income with Products and Tools of the Trade   **109**

Double Your Income with Products   109
   Tips to Create Products that Generate Income   109
   What Can You Sell? Profitable Products and Materials   113
   Profit from Handouts, Workbooks, and Customization   116
   Ways to Sell More Products   119
   Ways to Sell Your Products: Affiliate Online Programs   127

Tools of the Trade for Speakers, Trainers,
  and Consultants   127
   The Presentation: Your Best Marketing Tool   128
   Topics and Titles that Sell   129
   Designing Marketing Tools to Boost Your Income   132
   What Goes in Great Promotional Packages   134
   More Great Ideas for Your Promotional Kits   143

5. Remember   **144**

How Do You Keep From Giving Up?   144

Persistence and Tenacity   145

Life After Speaking, Consulting, and Training:
  What's the Next Step?   145

The Future of the Professional Training, Speaking,
  and Consulting World   146

Hold This in Your Heart   147

Bonus Checklist to Be the Best Professional
  They Ever Hired   147
   If Not You, Who?   147
   Long Before You Arrive   148
   Delayed Travel   154
   After You Arrive (Well Before the Presentation)   155
   As the Audience Begins to Come In   160
   Ten Minutes Before You Go On   161
   When You Step Up to the Lectern   161
   During the Presentation   161
   Right After the Presentation   162
   After You Go Home   163
   How to Recognize a Suspicious Parcel   163
Glossary of Speaking Terms   167
Index   199

Introduction

I, and others, like to claim we give you thousands of great ideas in our books. This book proves the case!

Throughout our lives, we hear millions of ideas. Some we grab onto and hold in our minds; they drive us forward. These are those great "keepers"! In my position as a speakers' bureau executive, an author, a seminar leader, and a speaker, I have the privilege of working with thousands of great speakers, trainers, and consultants. They have freely shared their great keeper ideas in the many surveys and books I have written. This book takes the best of those ideas, sorts them, and lists them out, one at a time, like this:

1. Most paid professional experts go through a stage of insanity when they try to be all things to all potential income sources. As you go through the hundreds of income-generating ideas in this book, avoid the insanity by focusing on only those ideas for which you can create the right fit with *your* abilities and *your* expertise.

2. More important, grab those ideas that seize you with a feeling of excitement! Those are the ideas for which you will add the most important aspect of all in making any idea work—drive.

In this book, each of the ideas has the potential to be the best income-generating idea you have ever used. Each idea has been tried by some and found to be fantastic! **Warning:** It has also been tried by others and found to be a miserable waste of time!

Why? Because the idea *inspired* some. They gave it the energy needed to turn it from words on paper to an income-generating stroke of genius. I include as many ideas as possible in the hopes that you will find the magic hundred or so that will inspire you and give you direction in increasing your income.

WHERE DID I FIND 1001 WAYS TO MAKE MORE MONEY AS A SPEAKER, CONSULTANT, OR TRAINER?

I have been employed in this industry since 1985, speaking, training, and consulting. I have gathered many tips and made plenty of mistakes as I went along. Also, I have gathered every good idea from all of my previous books and my *Speaking Industry Reports,* created from my surveys of thousands in our profession:

- 6500 professional speakers, trainers, humorists, or seminar leaders who are currently making at least $1000 per engagement, and who do at least 40 presentations a year at those fees. The majority of those responding to the survey are in a much higher fee range, but these were the minimum requirements.

- 400 meeting planners, from those who plan for one small company meeting to those planning hundreds of events per year.

- 300 speakers' bureaus that book speakers at all levels, from the $1,000 to $100,000 range.

DO YOU KNOW ENOUGH TO READ THIS BOOK?

This book assumes you have already at least made an entry into the world of speaking, consulting, and training. If you find yourself reading the 1001 ways I have for you here and going, "Huh?", then you need to read *Speak and Grow Rich* (Prentice Hall, 2002).

3.   Some of the ideas in this book are going to seem just too basic for you. Beware! Unless you are making $500,000 a year and are happy with the amount of your income (and if you are, why did you buy this book?), then you especially need to rethink those *basics* of marketing and boosting your income.

ARE THERE REALLY 1001 WAYS IN THIS BOOK WITH WHICH YOU CAN BOOST YOUR INCOME? DUPLICATES?

When you are looking for ways to profit from your writing skills, I mention e-zines. When we talk about ways to use your Web site, I tell you to allow a way for people to subscribe to your e-zine right at the site. Same method, different application.

You will see that many times I repeat that you need to listen to what your customer is telling you. I mention this when speaking directly to clients, when talking to speakers' bureaus, and when working with an audience. Several times, and in several contexts, I tell you to look at ways to pull business from those sitting in your audience.

I do not want you looking through the entire book when you want ideas on a specific subject.

4.   Yes! There are duplicates. Take these as a sign that I feel that idea is very important and well worth repeating. If you want something remembered in a presentation, plan on repeating it at least six times.

Wait! Are there really 1001 ways in this book?
In fact, there are . . .
well, wait until you read the last idea!

Income Streams

INCOME SOURCES FOR SPEAKERS, TRAINERS, OR CONSULTANTS
Let Us Count the Ways Experts Generate Income

Every beginning speaker, trainer, or seminar leader at first assumes the majority of his or her income should come from speaking engagements. However, the industry average shows that only 53 percent of your income will come from speaking engagements.[1]

There are many avenues of opportunity available through which experts can earn income through their knowledge.

5. Often, repackaging an old service you already offer—for instance, changing online training to a "24-hour information hotline" or renaming a self-study program "Just-in-Time training"—can open a whole new income stream up for you.

Ramon Williamson, a speaker, told me, "I get booked over and over now because of the value I give outside the speech. For example, I'll sell a keynote for $5000. I give a cassette for pre work and do a follow-up telecoaching call for the entire team. I usually get at least 6 to 10 private coaching clients out of the deal at $500 per month and I get invited back for refreshers at least twice in the same year. I earn $10,000 more in

---

[1] Lilly Walters, *Speaking Industry Reports.*

speaking fees and $20,000 to 30,000 for the coaching over the course of a year."

That is the type of mindset this book is going to help you create.

This chapter will outline only some of the categories you can work on as delivery methods for your help and expertise to the marketplace.

6.   As technology changes and your experience grows, we can arguably say the list of categories to boost your income is endless! As you read each idea I have here for you, write down the many more that will come as one idea inspires another.

Having a few or even all of the categories in this chapter available to your customers will generate no income unless you . . .

7.   Become an expert in subjects the market is asking for.

8.   Ask for business! "Ask and you shall receive!"

9.   Find ways to show your customers that you offer multiple ways to teach and help solve their challenges: each of these will be an income source.

10.   Create a menu of services, often called a fee schedule. Throughout this book will be many ideas. As you go through, add the ones you see as a match for your areas of expertise onto the menu of what you offer. People will never buy if they do not know what you sell and the many ways you can help them learn.

Authoring and Other Products

11.   There are many ways to profit from your writing skills. Many of the ideas in this book center around your creation of things you will initially write out, either as a speech outline, workbook, article, and so on. These things then become other types of products. (See Chapter 4.)

12.   One of the most valuable books to increase your income in this industry is the one you write yourself! Few things position you as well as writing a book.

Public Seminars

13.   The highest incomes available in this industry, other than for a very small handful of megacelebrities—such as former U.S. presidents—are to be made by hosting your own seminars. (See the entire section on this later in this chapter.)

Expert Witness Reports

14.   An expert witness is often called to appear on television and radio shows and in the print media for an expert comment on a situation. This leads to being paid to appear as an expert in court cases, and to training and speeches. An expert witness might also create a written document to be used in the case.

15.   Check with your reference librarian at the public library for current directories of expert witnesses and get listed.

16.   Search the Internet for expert witness sites and get listed with them.

17.   Offer to give free speeches to groups of attorneys on your area of expertise.

Infomercial Host

18.   As an infomercial host, you are paid a fee or a percentage of sales for this work. Sometimes your own book may be part of what is sold on the infomercial; sometimes the producers are just looking for a dynamic personality to host the program.

Commercials

19.   Some speakers are featured in commercials for the clients for whom they present programs.

20.   Trade your speaking/training skills with media in return for commercials for yourself.

Keynote Speeches

21.   Offer to do the keynote speech. Convention keynote session speakers have the highest visibility of all presenters because they appear before the entire assemblage. Often the keynote address is given by a celebrity speaker, or at least someone of renown to the particular audience—for instance, the president of an organization. The keynote normally requires the greatest level of skill as a presenter and is normally the highest-paid position at a convention.

Breakouts and Concurrent Sessions

22.   If giving the keynote, offer to do one, or even several, breakout sessions. In breakout sessions, the main group of attendees is divided into several concurrent sessions to hear special material on differing special-interest topics.

23.   Often you will have greater opportunity for networking with members of your audience during a breakout, as these sessions are much more personal and interactive than keynotes. More personal networking means more opportunity for you to find prospects in your audience. (See the section "Cultivating Sales, Repeats, Spin-offs, and Referrals" in Chap. 3.)

Master of Ceremonies

24.   Offer to be the master of ceremonies for events. A good master of ceremonies (emcee or MC) will fill the downtime on the stage, announce the sponsors, and keep the entire event moving along smoothly. Your comments will connect the separate sessions at the meeting together. The MC is almost always very funny. As MC, you would handle stage scheduling and stage managing. You would make the event run smoothly and keep it focused and successful. You keep the group focused and full of energy in between speakers at multiday meetings, creating a feeling of congruity. You would meet with clients in advance to gain a thorough knowledge of the intent of the event. It would be your responsibility to custom-tailor material suitable to the client, and to keep material this client would find offensive off of the platform.

If your wit is quick, and you can handle quick changes in program without letting the audience know there is ever a problem, then consider adding this to your fee schedule.

25. You might also act as the introducer for the other presenters. An introducer may or may not be the MC of the event. Specifically, the introducer introduces other presenters and leads the audience into a look within the speaker's history.

Panel Moderator

26. Offer your services as a panel moderator on your fee schedule. Many programs include one or several panels on topics that fit the theme and concerns of the audience. These can occur at conventions, retreats, or any sort of meeting where experts discussing an issue are valuable. You and other speakers may each be booked to present 10-minute speeches on a panel. Sometimes a Q&A session is offered so that the audience can ask the panelists questions.

Panel Coordinator and Creator

27. Offer to find other experts for the panel for a small additional fee. Since you are already an expert on your subject, you are a terrific resource for finding others.

Panel Participant

28. Offer your services as a panel participant on your own fee schedule.

29. Set your fee for being a panel participant at less than you charge for being a panel moderator.

Game Show Host for Meeting Events

30. You can create a game show and host it for your attendees. The attendees are the contestants. They answer questions and earn points for their team.

Games that bring the company's objectives and goals into focus are the most popular. You might accomplish this by having teams buy vowels or blurting out answers. You find ways to make it entertaining and challenging with Hollywood-style showmanship. You will create and supply a game show set with whatever graphics, music, bells, and whistles you feel are needed to create the ambience. You might also create Las Vegas–style casino party, or a murder mystery.

Partner (Spouse) Programs

31.   Offer special programs for spouses, partners, guests, and significant others of convention registrants. Many spouses today want to attend the sessions their partner is attending; others want programs specific to them. Many attendees want more opportunities to include the family and more emphasis on learning.

32.   Design your promotional materials to reflect your understanding of the specific needs of spouses. If you have taken the time to truly understand an industry, the chances are very good you will understand the challenges faced by spouses and can design a program perfectly suited to enrich and entertain them.

33.   Take a survey of 20 or more of the spouses of those in your industry to discover their specific needs and challenges.

Youth Programs

34.   Offer special programs for children of convention registrants.

35.   Take a survey of 20 or more parents. Ask them what they feel would best benefit their children, should they attend meetings.

36.   Design your promotional materials to reflect the parents' perception of which topics would best enrich and entertain their children.

37.   Contact schools and youth groups to offer your youth programs.

Pre or Post Programs

38. Offer to do a program before or after the convention. These programs are business-related programs for which attendees pay an additional fee to participate.

39. If you offer to do a pre or post program for a percentage of the fee the group is getting, the group is much more likely to hire you.

Pre or Post Locale Tours

40. If you are an expert on a locale, offer to conduct the tour laced with interesting facts about the area. To make a convention more enticing and exciting, tours are often offered in your local area. If you enjoy history and have been giving tours to your out-of-town relatives anyway, then why not get paid to offer tours to meetings that come to your area? Any time you can do a meeting in your local area, your relatives save on airfare and you get to eat dinner with your family!

Local Historical Characters

41. You might be able to create a business-related topic based on your knowledge of a famous historical character who has some connection to the local area. Some of the most famous business books have been based on famous people from history: Attila The Hun; Sun Tzu's *The Art of War* (which by the way was the number four best-seller the day I wrote this for you!). What famous historical figures are associated with your area? What were/are their philosophies? This could easily be the makings of a terrific best-seller for you.

Entertainment

42. Create and offer an entertainment program. This is a nonmessage act such as dance bands, jugglers, magicians, comedians.

Add-on Event Ideas: Pictures

43. Since you are there anyway, think of other services the event planner might like to offer to make the meeting more fun or educational or to help people network better.

44.   Take slides or videos of participants at an event the day before. Create a show to be shown at a cocktail party, or while the participants are eating. Taking these pictures is a great way to network with people while you are there. The completed project creates a great entertainment option for them.

45.   Take pictures of people and use their voices transferred to WAV files on the computer.

46.   Create a photo or video album of their event. This can be used after the event as a special gift for the attendees.

Training

47.   The training field is one of the largest areas of opportunity for professional speakers. Normally training implies more than a half-day session. Most often it implies several days or even weeks. Training can be offered in many ways, in the form of a seminar, Just-in-Time training, or many other methods you will read about in this book. Be prepared: you will discover many more as you work with people in your industry and discover their needs.

You may already be offering a seminar or workshop. Perhaps you are a consultant who gives a manual to your clients as part of your service. You may already be giving training sessions to your customers, but calling it something else. Training can and should be a separately itemized entity on your fee schedule.

But remember, *training* implies attendees will leave your program with a set of skills they did not formerly possess.

In-House Seminars and Workshops

48.   In-house seminars and workshops are often thought to be half-day to full-day sessions. This is often perceived as a much different type of program than training, and can be listed as a separate item. If your market is the type that can normally only allow for a half-day program, consider offering a seminar or workshop.

Moderator or Facilitator

49. Many presenters are paid to simply moderate or facilitate discussions. Offer to have groups do interactive exercises, then simply listen and direct the conversation afterward, or debrief.

50. Direct problem-solving sessions. This is often done for a small group of executives who are having trouble getting over an issue.

Consultant

51. Frequently companies need special help with a problem. This is where a consultant comes in. Offer consulting in several formats, such as traditional standalone consulting, by-the-hour consulting; going out in the field with the client's salespeople; or monitoring incoming calls, then preparing a presentation. Often a consultant can stay at home more often than a speaker does, because much of the consultant's work is done back at his or her home office. Consulting takes much longer, but is usually a much larger contract than a single speaking engagement.

52. Being a consultant who speaks has very different focus that might make you seem even more of an expert and therefore worth a higher fee than a speaker or trainer who consults.

53. Suggest to your customers that a preestablished training course might not be the best solution to their challenges. Suggest that you can evaluate their problems and offer concrete, customized suggestions for improvement. This is the essence of consulting.

54. Offer follow-up consulting after a speech to check the progress of the attendees, either as an add-on value to your package or for an additional fee. Often attendees feel they hear a presenter and then are left to perhaps improve, perhaps not. If you offer a consulting service that will assess the progress of what the attendees learned, and make suggestions on how they can improve, it is of tremendous value.

Work for a Consulting Firm

55.   In addition to all of the ways mentioned in the book to boost income as a consultant, here are a few more specific to consultants. Do an Internet search using Google keyword *consulting*. You will see about 12,400,000 places come up. Then, scroll to the link that says SEARCH WITHIN THESE RESULTS and type in your area of expertise. Go to the first 50 results and see if they have a link for careers or jobs.

56.   Go to the major job finder sites on the Internet: Monster.com, Careerbuilders.com, and many others. Use the keywords *consultant* and your area of expertise.

57.   Call the local consultants in your area. They might be willing to use you when they are overloaded.

58.   Check with associations of consultants, network with them, and offer to assist them.

One-on-One Executive Trainer

59.   You will be surprised at the number of executives who want private, one-on-one training. Rightly or wrongly, they do not want the team to see the areas in which they are seeking to increase their competency. Nor do they want the program to be perceived as the same program the troops receive. Include executive one-on-one trainer on your menu of services with topics aimed at executives' needs.

Coach

60.   Coaching is a system of skill and attitude improvement that is usually more one-on-one than consulting. Coaching in general is thought to be aimed at many levels of employees, rather than just the executive. Some coaches are former CEOs of Fortune 1000 companies. These types of coaches will charge $4000 or more a month to be on retainer as a coach for an individual.

61. In addition to offering coaching in person, also offer it via phone, fax, and e-mail. Some people will be much more ready to buy when they know they can stay in their own home or office and still receive their coaching without travel.

62. Offer coaching for personal skill and attitude improvement for a monthly or per-call fee. The coaching fee might be set per hour or by the month. Coaches charge around $300 and up per month for being available for phone calls and e-mail.

63. Offer to be an on-the-job coach for businesses. You might actually go out with the sales crew on calls to their customers, or sit in on telephone sales groups inside a company. This is fieldwork to discover problems.

64. Offer telephone group discussion sessions periodically to coach.

65. Assign partners among your clients to assist each other as add-on value. By coaching each other, they gain a great deal of knowledge, and you have all kinds of assistants.

66. Help your coaching clients form mastermind groups. Mastermind groups are a great way to solve problems and to bounce your ideas off of others. By establishing these groups for your coaching clients, you give them a fantastic resource that takes very little on your part to maintain.

Conference Calls

67. Add conference calls as part of your consulting or training package. A conference call is a problem-solving session where the content is fluid.

68. Add conference calls as a follow-up add-on benefit after a workshop or other programs. A conference call can be billed as a mini-seminar.

Creating a Hotline Service

69.   A hotline, although it entails no more than you being available 24/7 via telephone, is perceived as something much different than your normal cell phone. This perception is a billable commodity. A hotline enables your customers to find emergency assistance and advice with their challenges. Knowing help is close at hand is a very valuable resource, one that many are willing to pay for.

70.   A hotline, like many other services, might be a service you give away, but one whose worth you will list on the invoice with a specific value, then show that it has been thrown in as part of a reduced package fee.

After-Hours Tutor

71.   Calling one of your services after-hours tutoring lets your clients know they do not need to pull their teams off of their tasks if they use you as a coach, consultant, or trainer. This also comes under distance education ideas (see later in this chapter).

Company Training Films and Videos

72.   Associations and companies create training videos and/or CD-ROMs. Offer to be the narrator for them.

73.   Offer to create, produce, and possibly even narrate a video training program for a company. When you produce a program, you handle all details, such as hiring the actors, renting the camera, writing, and finding a script writer. When done for a company, this is done to meet your unique goals and objectives.

Sponsors

Find a sponsor. A sponsor pays you by the event, on a retainer, or by an advertisement in your materials. Sometimes sponsors are retailers, sometimes manufacturers of products.

74.   If your heart's desire is to present to audiences that have little or no funds, then find a sponsor who also is trying to reach that market. For instance, a sponsor might want a way to reach schoolchildren. Your program might also be great for children. Schools have less than little money, so the sponsor pays your way instead of the school. Depending on your topic, providers of sporting goods, shoes, and so on might be very interested in sponsoring you.

75.   Find a sponsor to buy an ad in the inside of your workbook. You can place half-page ads in appropriate spots in your workbook, such as those sections where you talk about the sponsor's kind of product.

76.   Find sponsors that you are already promoting. For example, if you believe that using a planner of some type is essential to your audience's success with your philosophies, then seek sponsorship from those you feel are the best manufacturers of those planners. If that manufacturer says no, then check out the hundreds of others that make very similar products.

77.   Find sponsors that want a link on your Web site back to theirs.

78.   Find sponsors that want links in your e-news.

Spokesperson

79.   Companies often look for speakers who can act as spokespersons for their products, services, or public image. The speaker may travel to many areas, present speeches and seminars, and often participate in media interviews or personal appearances to promote the sponsoring organization's products, services, or image. Contact the large corporations or organizations in your area of expertise who relate to and need your topic. You would be the representative of the client's customers or patients.

80.   Approach those who sell to your target market. They may be the most interested in using you as a spokesperson.

Seminars to Promote a Client

81.   Approach companies whose customers would benefit from your subject. Suggest they pay you to give a workshop or seminar as a way of pulling customers in the door. Retailers such as Price/Costco, Staples, Sears, Nordstrom, and many others advertise and promote seminars for their customers, usually held in their stores. Banks, craft stores, and all kinds of companies offer these types of seminars to the public. They need to hire speakers who are experts to present seminars to these customers.

82.   List everything you do on your menu of services. They will not buy it if they do not know that you sell it! (Yes, this is a duplicate idea. Please note I have duplicated it because of its extreme importance to your success in this industry.)

HIRE YOURSELF: PUBLIC SEMINARS AND EVENTS

83.   Create your own public seminar, and hire yourself as the speaker! This way you never need to worry about where your next booking is coming from.

Public seminars have the highest profit and the highest risk of any enterprise in this industry. Public seminars are sold to the public (individuals) rather than to corporations or associations. Weekend seminars, for example, often are marketed at $1500 per attendee per event. Multiply that figure by 200 participants and you get a gross income of $300,000 for a two-day weekend retreat. This level of income, and more, is fact, not fiction.

84.   Often corporations look for public seminars to send their people to when they have a need for training, but they either can't release larger numbers of people at one time or they only need a few of their people trained in the specific topic area. The types of topics offered in public seminars are limitless, from how to get a date to how to build a computer.

Filling the Seats

85. Publicity stories and other promotional ideas will bring in numbers. (See the entire section "Promotional Strategies" in Chap. 3.)

86. Target your seminar to appeal to a specialized market.

87. Target your promotional ideas to appeal to a specialized market.

88. Only advertise in magazines, trade publications, and newsletters specific to your target market.

89. Use newspaper and radio advertising to reach your market if your topic is generic.

90. Use direct mail to specific markets. There are many companies that sell direct mail and e-mail lists.

91. Start a newsletter and/or e-zine aimed at your market, filled with informative, educational, must-know information. Mail (or e-mail) it to your prospective attendees at least twice a year.

92. Publish an updated calendar of your upcoming seminars. Have it posted on your Web site, and have a printed version available at all times. Give prospects a choice of places and dates; this increases the chance that they will register for your seminar. Listing a series of dates also lets prospects know you are successful at what you offer.

93. Whenever you speak—for a public seminar or private client—your calendar should be given out as a single-page handout slipped into your printed handout materials. State on the calendar if a date is open to the public, and have a phone number to contact to sign up for each event.

94. List your public seminar topics and dates with online services. Search the Internet for sites that will list your seminar.

95. Many newspapers have a seminar section where you can advertise the seminars you sell to the public.

96. Develop a mailing list, fax number list, and e-mail list of your own from every attendee and inquiry. I find that 75 percent of seminar attendees come through recommendations from past attendees.

97. Consider trading mailing lists or plugs with others who offer seminars on topics related to yours.

98. Try the two-step, a set of two seminars. At the first seminar, which is free, give such great value, and create such excitement, that attendees want to sign up for the second, more valuable (and for a fee) course.

Products at Public Seminars

99. Create a store at the back of the room with your products and other items that will help your attendees benefit from your topic.

100. In your store, sell other experts' materials on your subject. People will see two or three of the mega-superstars on your subject, and *you!* They will quickly associate you with these great names on the subject. Most publishers are glad to offer you their materials at 30 to 50 percent off retail.

101. You can charge more for your seminar if you include a "bundle" of products.

Phone Seminars

102. Offer phone/tele-seminars as one of many methods of delivering information. A phone seminar is given at a set time; each participant calls in and logs into the group. You market the program just as you would any other public seminar. You send your workbooks out to the participants prior to the event; this can even be done via e-mail.

Working with Public Seminar Producers

103. If you work with someone else who will produce your seminar, your profit will be less, but so will your risk. They produce the seminar, and you just show up, speak, and sell product. You are paid a flat fee (much smaller than you will receive for corporate or association work) with a cut of product sales.

Usually, public seminar companies contract with you to present a seminar whose content is owned by the seminar company. The seminar's subject may or may not be one that you have had experience with previously. Some of the more famous public seminar companies are Fred Pryor/CareerTrack, National Seminars, and Dun & Bradstreet, but there are many others, all with various ways of doing business.

Share the Gate

104. The types of companies that will host a public seminar on a "share-the-gate" basis are almost endless. Look at any business or association that might want to increase its visibility or make use of a facility that is not full seven days a week. Go to every group within 100 miles of your home that might want to share the gate. Suggest that you offer at least two programs a year for them—perhaps a first program for beginners, and a follow-up or advanced program.

Building relationships with 20 groups is rather simple. That's about one booking a week, a good start. Any group interested in increasing revenue likely will listen to your proposition for a seminar project, especially if it is closely suited to the group's members. The trick is to find the groups that will tie in best with your subject and that have a mailing list to which they already send mail regularly.

All of the following types of groups offer fundraising classes that complement their aims and help promote them.

105. Churches

106. PTAs

107. School booster clubs

108. Hospitals

109. Chambers of commerce

110.   Economic Development Centers

111.   Service clubs (Rotary, Kiwanis, Lions, etc.)

112.   Associations that wish to offer their members semi-nars and are glad to book them on a share-the-gate basis

113.   Local television stations

114.   Newspapers

115.   Radio shows

116.   Colleges and universities offer noncredit classes, especially at junior college facilities. Your local colleges are already sending their catalogs of credit classes out to a huge geographic area local to you and them. These include a section in the back for noncredit classes on all kinds of topics. You would hold the class right on campus.

117.   Urban independent seminar companies have you deliver your own seminar. You split the gate and sell products. The most famous of this type of company is the Learning Annex. You find these types of companies most often by looking in those places where free catalogs are given away by newsstands, in your mailbox, and on the Internet.

Enhancing Income
With Share-the-Gate Seminars

118.   Create spin-off business from your public seminar. Attendees may be employees of companies who might be part of a big chain or industry you had not thought to market to. So you are off and running with a whole new set of prospects and markets by sharing the gate!

119.   When you establish successful co-op relationship with one organization, you will be ready to move on to more groups. Ask the group you had success with for three things: A letter of recommendation; a list of other groups affiliated with them, such as other churches of the same denomination or other chapters nationwide or worldwide, and a contact name there; and a list of which associations they belong to. When you know which associations they belong to, you will have a great additional source to which you can market yourself. These association dates will often be fee-paid dates rather than share-the-gate.

Adventures, Seminars at Sea, and Resorts

120.   You can create a learning-filled, fun, and exotic seminar in any location. Create an adventure seminar: Attendees can sign up for a safari in Kenya, join a cattle drive in Montana, go scuba diving in the Red Sea, learn lessons about life by flying a fighter jet. Even at a local hotel, the presenters can create an atmosphere of adventure with team-building games and ambience. The group members work together and challenge their limits through a series of activities you create and coordinate.

121.   You may be able to resell tickets to a cruise or rooms at the resort to your attendees, and make a commission on those from the venue at the same time you sell registrations to your seminar.

122.   Share the gangplank and sell tickets as a public seminar at sea. Cooperate with cruise companies.

123.   Hold your seminars at sea by exchanging your programs for a working vacation. Contact the cruise ship companies to be one of their two or three enrichment speakers per trip for regular vacationers.

Continuing Education Marketplace

124.   Continuing education units (CEUs) are often required by licensed professionals in order to maintain their license. These credits are awarded for taking classes approved by the licensing body of the state and/or organization that requires continuing education units. Professional organizations for lawyers, many in the medical field, polygraph examiners, and thousands of others insist on their members taking these classes. Go to those already in your target market and ask which group gives them their accreditation. Contact that group and ask how you could be on the list of seminar presenters. Topics they use are varied. Those in the medical field take ongoing classes on medical issues, but also in general topics, such as leadership and handling difficult people or patients.

Virtual Seminars: Correspondence School to Net Classrooms

125.   You can increase your income by having virtual seminars that combine the traditional correspondence school format, e-mail, and/or live chat. Some seminars also require students to use offline resources such as books, audios, and videos. The many ways these seminars can be given are limited only by your imagination, and today's technology, which will be even better tomorrow!

We may well be calling this the "Death of Distance Decade!" We are a society that has learned to expect an instant business response. The idea that you must wait to train your team until the classroom or the presenter is available is not always the best choice.

No or few travel costs are involved in virtual programs. Attendees don't have to commute or relocate. Virtual seminars extend your geographic reach. Students can be in the next room, another state, or another country, all at the same time, or at any time they want.

126.   Updating electronic books and workbooks for virtual seminars is simple and costs a fraction of the production expense for normal paper materials. You can keep your materials current because you do not need to worry about actual heavy costs of paper workbooks and other materials.

Just-in-Time Training Programs

127.   Many buyers look for Just-in-Time Training, meaning they want it when they want it and how they want it, and in whatever bite-size pieces they are able to take in at the time. These are self-study programs to deliver your training. These work without you being there at all.

This is really the same as calling the process a virtual seminar or distance learning. However, in some cases the packaging of a Just-in-Time method of teaching can create a higher perceived value than other methods. Poll your customers to see if your title or another has greater perceived value. Then explore why and how you can tailor your program to meet their greatest appreciated value.

Distance Learning

128.   Distance learning is a term most commonly used in the academic community. Implied is more actual involvement from the instructor. A distance learning system gives attendees methods of learning such as self-directed, practice-based, problem-based learning; small group discussion; and audit of assignments. Supplement these when possible with supervised practice, periodic audio teleconferencing, multimedia self-learning packages, weekend courses and regular assessments, telephone counseling at any time, and Web site visits. Calling your program distance learning may give it a higher perceived value with your customer base. Ask!

Teleconferencing, Videoconferencing, and Desktop Conferencing

129.   Help your customers envision alternative ways of receiving information by including teleconferencing, videoconferencing, and desktop conferencing on your fee schedule.

130.   Offer your virtual class through other online places: AOL and many Web sites offer a virtual university where you offer your class.

FREE SPEAKING: PROFITING FROM NON-FEE PRESENTATIONS

131.   The majority of speeches in the world are done for no fee. Obviously, there are many benefits of speaking for no fee, or so many people wouldn't be doing them! Get out there and talk to any group that will listen.

132.   It is better to do something for nothing than nothing for nothing.

Benefits of Nonfee Presentations

133.   Correct performance problems: use no-fee engagement as the perfect laboratory to become the best! Even top comedians such as Robin Williams and Joan Rivers try out new material at comedy clubs to test audience reaction.

134.   Exposure and publicity: use free (and paid) speeches for publicity. Send press releases out to the media that state you are speaking to a prestigious group. Make sure to mention the name of your book.

135.   Educate the public: contact large companies. Many realize that tremendous marketing and goodwill benefits are available to them when they send presenters out to the public to teach about their product and industry.

136.   Arrange for a way to sell your products at the back of the room.

137.   Contact bookstores that bring in speakers for book signings to give your talk for free, but you sell your products.

138.   Arrange for a way to sell your services at the back of the room to obtain prospective clients. Many a business is sustained by this method. Attorneys may speak to business audiences about "How to Avoid Probate" or "How to Keep Your Company out of Court Because of Wrongful Firing of Employees." A plastic surgeon, using before-and-after slides as illustrations, speaks to a sales organization about new surgical techniques to improve appearance.

139.   Create opportunities for paid bookings: you know you are good when someone in your no-fee audience comes up to you and asks you what your fee would be to speak for their event.

Ways to Find Paying Customers in Your Nonfee Talks

140.   No-fee presentations can help you obtain bookings, especially if members of associations and corporations are in your target market. Cultivate them.

141.   See the section "Cultivating Sales, Repeats, Spin-offs, and Referrals" in Chap. 3.

Service Clubs

142.   Service clubs are always on the lookout for those wishing to speak for their local meetings. These organizations hold weekly meetings at different times of the day. Some are breakfast clubs, some are luncheon groups, and others always meet in the evening. There are often many chapters of the same service club, such as the Rotary, in the same city. Many of those who belong to service clubs are employees of other businesses who might be able to book you.

143.   Although local service clubs are often looking for a no-fee speaker, for their regional events they will usually pay the speaker a fee.

144.   Join service clubs in your area; get involved at the national level by belonging to different committees.

Look in These Places to Find Service Clubs

145.   The Internet: try Yahoo!, because their sites are organized in categories rather than just a keyword list. Try searching under *community organizations.*

146.   Your local library: ask the reference librarian for help in locating service clubs.

147.   Your phone book and online phone books, such as Superpages.com.

148.   Your local chamber of commerce will know which service groups are in your area.

149.   Local newspapers often contain notices of when these groups meet.

150. Call local hotels and restaurants with banquet rooms; ask the manager what other groups meet regularly in the venue.

151. Ask the chapter you are currently speaking for if you can have a copy of the roster or directory of other chapters.

152. Ask your business friends and clients if they are members of various business service clubs. Ask for the name and phone number of the president of the club.

153. Try Google.com for clubs.

Who to Look for

154. The most famous are the Rotary, Lions, Kiwanis, and the Jaycees. But there are many other service organizations in your area. Check the sources listed previously to find them.

More Ways to Give It Away— And Profit!

155. You get back what you give out. Always be ready to offer help and advice. Be known as the person with *solutions!*

156. Offer your free help and advice with limits. Never let those who are paying you suffer for those who are not.

157. Do an extremely good job if are you doing work for free. Never give it a half-effort because there is no fee.

Those Who Buy
and Why

WHERE, WHY, AND HOW BUYERS WILL BUY YOU!

Where Do You Find Buyers?

This entire book is about ways to reach buyers and close bookings. Here are some more duplicate ideas from other spots in the book that deal specifically with where to look for buyers.

158. Direct your marketing at associations with conferences who have CEOs as attendees. These are great sources of leads should you be able to speak for them.

159. Join and become involved in associations. This creates friends, who are then more likely to refer you.

160. Go to an Internet search engine and try this phrase: *schedule of events meeting keynote speaker,* then add in your target market—for instance, *plumbers.*

161. Frequent places attended by decision makers—perhaps annual awards night at local chamber of commerce or charity events and so on.

162. Speak free for the local Rotary, chambers of commerce, and other service clubs. Become involved, especially by attending the yearly goals conference.

163.   Offer your program as a fund raiser for social and professional organizations to which senior managers may belong.

164.   One or more buyers will be watching and listening at each speech you give. Seek them out. (See the section "Cultivating Sales, Repeats, Spin-offs, and Referrals" in Chap. 3.)

165.   Ask the reference librarian at the library to assist you. There are local, state, and national directories for virtually every kind of business and association.

166.   Look among friends and acquaintances of the buyer who is your current client.

167.   Look among groups related to your current buyers. Build your connections laterally. For example, if you began with banking, approach buyers for banks in the same company first, then buyers at other banks. Work citywide, then statewide, then nationally.

168.   What does your current customer read? Find out and write articles for those publications.

169.   Look at the news for your potential buyers. By capitalizing on your observations of the issues your target industry faces, you will be able to find a sponsor for a seminar, do a joint venture in advertising, or find a client who needs a training session.

170.   Study advertisements. They are full of prospects. Watch for businesses, hospitals, or any other type of group offering seminars to its clients. Call and ask if the group might like to use your subject for its next promotional event.

Showcases

A showcase is an event that allows buyers to audition several speakers in one session. Most noncelebrity speakers pay a fee for their slot on the showcase program, which is a little like a fashion show. Buyers come to look, listen, and book.

There are many showcases offered to speakers that are sponsored by groups like the following.

171.   Speakers' bureaus

172.   Speakers' associations (usually at the local level)

173.   The National Association of Campus Activities (NACA)

174.   Meeting Professionals International (MPI)

175.   The American Society of Association Executives (ASAE)

176.   The International Association of Speakers Bureaus

177.   Showcases you create yourself, bringing in other complementary but not competing presenters and experts. You will all pool your mailing lists and do one large mailing to all of them.

Ways to Make All Types of Showcasing Profitable

178.   There are many ways to showcase your abilities to potential buyers. This is called showcasing. In addition to watching you perform, consider that every time you are not alone, you are showcasing not only your potential as a paid expert but your abilities as a communicator and your character. Often presenters are passed over because a potential buyer has seen the presenter off stage in a rage over a personal issue.

179.   Network and invite people to come see you perform who are in a position to pay you for your expertise and talents.

180.   Invite speakers' bureaus to hear your programs when you are in their geographic area.

181.   Invite colleagues with whom you can share leads to come and see you speak or train.

182.   Never do free showcases unless you have a system set up by which you can gather referrals. (See Chap. 3.)

183.   When you do a free speech to showcase yourself, ask for an article in the publications that go to the organization's entire membership. Agree up front that this will include your contact information.

184.   When you do a free speech to showcase yourself, ask for a free large advertisement in the program.

185.   When you do a free speech to showcase yourself, ask for your contact information to be included in the program where your name and program description are located.

186.   Make sure you leave a trail of something for people to follow back to you: have your contact information on the handouts or other giveaways at your program.

Directories of Buyers

187.   Lilly Walters' Grand Master Hyperlink List of Speakers' Bureaus is the most up-to-date list of speakers' bureaus available. It includes over 400 bureaus around the world, their phone numbers, and links to their Web sites. See more at www.motivational-keynote-speakers.com.

188.   The staff of *Salesman's Guide,* published by Douglas New Reed Ref Publishing in New Providence, New Jersey, personally calls every member of many associations and corporations and asks whether they hire speakers. They compile this information and sell it in a directory for the use of speakers.

189.   Becoming involved in your target market and joining your client's association, will normally give you a directory of the membership to which you can direct your marketing.

**Ways to Get in Front of the Real
Decision Makers**

190.   First, find out the decision-making process involved in the buy decision. With each major purchase, often a committee will make the decision. In this case, your strategy would be to find ways to approach the committee while it is in session. Trying to sell members one at a time is much more difficult.

191.   The decision to hire a speaker, seminar leader, or trainer is usually not made by the meeting planner. The decision is often made by the meeting planner's boss, perhaps the president, vice president, executive director, or CEO. It is often best to target bulk marketing to people in these positions. In the case of business meetings, most often upper management makes the decision to hold the meeting. It is necessary to find the sponsor of the meeting and the theme. Customize your marketing material to emphasize their objectives.

192.   Executives often need convincing by the meeting planner that the presenter the planner likes is the person who will help the conference or meeting be outstanding. Therefore you should not ignore meeting planners in your marketing and manners. Sometimes the meeting planner has a title like director; then he or she may make the decision. With downsizing, the person coordinating the meeting planning is usually doing it as a sidebar to his or her real responsibilities, except in the biggest firms. Often the responsibility for the job of meeting planner changes yearly, which makes marketing to planners very difficult.

How to Penetrate Large Companies

The Approach

193.   You will very rarely be able to close a deal in one phone call. Develop a long-term approach to your marketing to large companies.

194.   It is much better to find ways to get the companies to call you, rather than you calling them.

195.   Carefully assess clients' needs, carefully listen to what they say those needs are, and take time to draft a comprehensive proposal that meets their perceived needs, with a flavoring of what you see as the solution to those needs and challenges.

196.   Explore ways to adjust your proposal so that it fits the client's particular audience culture and style. Get the buyer to help you achieve the right focus. For example, dentists have patients, attorneys have clients, salespeople have customers. Don't constantly refer to salesmen if a group also has saleswomen. Be aware of each group's problems and needs—and talk about them.

197. Create products that exactly meet the group's perceived needs and challenges.

198. Never tell group members they are in a bad way and need your information! Let them say that, you smile and downplay their problems, giving praise where you can.

199. Make your products and presentations an essential part of the group's corporate culture.

200. Create your materials so they can be used at many levels in a company: a set for entry level, middle management, and executive needs.

201. Cold-call the personnel manager to find out who books events, speakers, and trainers.

Use Articles to Reach Senior Managers

202. Write in high-level trade magazines.

203. Send articles you have written to the appropriate executives.

204. Write articles for the client's workplace newsletter and e-news.

Target Senior Managers

205. Start at the top—contact the CEO's office and ask him or her or the executive assistant who you should talk to.

206. Find out who the senior managers are, and mail them one of your books.

207. Target materials and events you send as specific for senior management teams. These are the people who will hire you for many more presentations and for consulting at other levels within the company.

Getting Referrals

See the section "Cultivating Sales, Repeats, Spin-offs, and Referrals" in Chap. 3.

208. Ask if someone who has heard you within a large business would act as a reference for you. Explain that this means giving out their phone number to a few potential clients who are wondering about your programs.

209. Talk with your customers one-on-one and assess their circle of influence; ask for a referral.

210. Ask your current customers if they would be willing to send an e-mail to potential internal leads.

Use Public Seminars

211. Teach part-time at the local university or college where the participants in continuing education come from many companies.

212. Know the jobs of all of attendees at your public seminars. Use your break and lunch times to talk with individuals in appropriate large companies about who they know and how to best approach those people.

213. People rarely keep flyers. Have your business card–size version of your program flyers available for people to take away at your public seminars.

More Ways to Penetrate Large Businesses

214. Build good relationships with speakers' bureaus.

215. Form alliances with other trainers/consultants in related fields to present a total package that is bigger than what you can do alone.

216. Target companies that handle the outsourcing of big companies' human resources.

217. Offer to do smaller in-house workshops or a free showcase. Write a contract stating that you will do the program if the decision maker for the larger events is invited and present.

218. Schedule time for marketing; aim for at least one day per week.

219. Offer a list of many exciting programs in modular standalone segments that will take weeks to accomplish. Often clients will hire you for more than just one day when they see all you have to offer.

220. Find marketing tactics in this book that work for you, and create a magic combination for your own needs.

For example: telephone qualification, a direct mail piece, telephone follow-up, and articles in publications clients read.

221.   Believe that what you have to offer is something clients need.

Why Buyers Like, Buy, and Dislike You

Clients Hire Who They Hire Because . . .

222.   You are hired first because of the message you give, next because you were referred by someone known and trusted by the person hiring who made a recommendation.

223.   Clients hire you because you know how to listen, and you find out what the buyer is looking for before going into the big sales pitch.

224.   You are hired because of a great demo tape (Read the section "Tools of the Trade for Speakers, Trainers, and Consultants" in Chap. 4.)

Clients Suggest You a Second Time Because . . .

225.   The audience loved you and wanted more.

226.   You are the same off-stage as on stage.

227.   You don't do any sales pitches for your products on the platform, or you do it so well, the audience appreciates the information.

228.   Before the event, you actually read the background information material the company provided.

229.   You are a pleasure to work with. You moved chairs if they needed to be moved and laughed at mishaps.

AGENTS, SPEAKERS' BUREAUS, AND MIDDLEMEN

230.   Middlemen are a viable source of income for professional speakers, trainers, seminar leaders, and consultants. *Once you are receiving solid and consistent fees for* *your bookings,* it is time to consider the advantages of working with those who sell speakers.

There are speakers' bureaus, agents, and brokers who work with many speakers, trainers, and seminar leaders. There is a great deal of overlap in what each one does. An agent, by definition, would work with a small number of people exclusively. Bureaus and brokers are much like travel agents. They work for the end buyer, are paid by a commission from the total fee, and have thousands of people in their databases to choose from.

To make this discussion easier, I will call all of these groups bureaus.

231. You will have the greatest success in any sales situation if you try to understand who you are selling to. A bureau could lose an important source of income by booking just one speaker who is not what the client wanted or who does not give a program that lives up to promises.

232. Bureaus not only search for the most talented speakers they can find, but they also watch closely for presenters who have the ability to be client pleasers and are a pleasure to work with.

233. To protect their investment, bureaus need presenters who understand the importance and fragility of their relationship with clients and potential clients and work to protect it.

Bureaus Dislike You Because . . .

234. When you are asked about your fees, you say, "Oh, it all depends . . .".

235. You have no dedicated fax line or computer line, and you make your phone line do double duty.

236. You do not read (or have someone else read) your e-mail.

237. You have call waiting.

238. You have not yet learned how to use e-mail, and cannot e-mail program outlines and photos.

239.   You do not yet have good promotional material, but you want the bureau to book you.

240.   When they try to tell you why they are not booking you, you reply, "No other bureaus think that's a problem!" (So why are you calling them?)

241.   You send them your materials COD!

242.   You think an affiliation with a club or association is *all* you need to be a professional—for example, "member of Toastmasters," "member of National Speakers Association," "member of American Society for Training and Development."

243.   You send them a carton of "stuff" unsolicited.

244.   You send them a letter saying, "In regards to our recent conversation . . ." when you have never actually spoken.

245.   You send them an article praising you, without a return address, and with a fictitious name signed in pen on the article saying something to the effect of, "This is great information! I heard him/her speak too, great job!"

246.   Your demo tape was done in front of a fake audience brought in for the purpose—or no audience at all.

247.   You tell a client to work directly with you instead of the bureau.

248.   You are aggressive or crude.

249.   You do not appreciate the difference in that an agent works for you. Brokers and speakers' bureaus work for the end buyer, like a travel agent, and work to find the right speaker for that buyer.

250.   Your expense reports are inconsistent with signed agreements.

251.   You take holds from a number of bureaus for the same date with the same client. The first bureau who places the hold should be honored.

252.   You have a lead-sharing group. Bureaus are immediately suspicious of this. Never share leads that come from a bureau.

253. You are just not good enough at the craft of speaking.

254. A client complained about your conduct in confidence to the bureau.

255. You approach them at busy conventions or meetings. If you meet them when they are busy, ask them the best time and way to contact them. Do so at their convenience.

256. You find a bureau agent at a cocktail party and you give them your 20 "best" minutes.

257. When they ask you what your topic is, you say, "Uh, well, you see, I have often been asked to speak on . . .". You have already lost them. You have about 15 seconds before they tune you out and start waiting for an appropriate opening to say good-bye.

258. You suggest other speakers to any client, or potential client, that has any connection to a speakers' bureau. If a client asks you, "Do you happen to know a speaker on ____?" or, "Do you know how I can reach ____?", say, "Certainly, (insert the name of the bureau that booked you) knows! I'll have them call you."

259. When you are asked for a package, you reply, "Well, you already have my ____ (bio, demo tape, article, whatever) there in your office. You know I sent it last month." The bureau will often reply, "Oh, OK, I'll go find it." What they are really saying is, "How do I get this person off of my phone and out of my life? I don't want to admit I trashed that package with all the others I didn't have time to preview!"

260. Your office staff is unprofessional or just plain annoying to work with. (Get them to read this book!)

261. You hand out your business cards at events. You should hand out the bureau's business cards.

262. You ask the client for a letter of recommendation on a bureau booking, then put it in your promotional kit for other bureaus.

You Annoy Bureaus When You Call Because . . .

263. You call to explain why your presentation is better than all the rest.

264. You can't tell the bureau what you speak about in one clear sentence.

265. You take more than 10 seconds to get to the point of your phone call.

266. You call them collect.

267. You tell the bureau in your sales call to them that you sell yourself and really do not require a bureau.

268. You call and interrupt the bureau's business more than once every three months.

269. You call during prime working hours when the bureau hopes to be talking to customers.

270. You can't tell the bureau in one sentence what differentiates you from the other 500 people who speak on the same topic.

271. You hire a scripted telemarketer to call the bureau.

272. Your attitude implies you are doing the bureau a great service or favor by allowing them to consider you.

273. You don't take the time to find out what the bureau's specialty is or the fee range of presenters they normally book. Find out this information by checking their Web site.

274. You call bureaus more often than they call you to make sure they think of you when leads come into your office.

275. You call for free advice on how to become a success in the speaking industry.

276. You or your staff members call a bureau and have no clue that you have met and spoken already on several occasions.

Brokers Are Impressed When You Try to "Sell" Them Because . . .

277. You have clear, clever, unique, yet benefit-specific marketing materials. (See "Tools of the Trade for Speakers, Trainers, and Consultants" in Chap. 4.)

278. You can tell them what you talk about in one sentence, and who the subject will best sell to in one more sentence. Combining it all into about 12 words is better yet!

279. You fill a niche in their roster that is needed by their customer base.

280. You are super-hyper-over-the-top careful about the way you track your leads.

281. You have a track record of paid bookings in the price range at which you want them to book you.

282. You equip the bureau with all the packaging necessary to represent yourself well.

283. You have a promotional tape that will attract interest from their customers.

284. You have bureau-friendly promotional materials (materials with no contact information).

285. Your fee range matches the bureau's clients' needs.

286. You keep your calls short and to the point; you know the points that will wow the bureau and you state them quickly.

287. You are unique, and you help the bureau see that uniqueness and clearly define what makes you different (being great will not make you different.)

288. Although you have an old topic, you present it in a new way that excites the bureau's customer base.

289. You are easy to get a hold of. You call back within minutes, not days.

290. You are easy and pleasant to work with.

291. You get bureaus exactly what they ask for, when they ask for it.

292. You give helpful follow-up, with no expectations.

293. You participate with them in another service they offer (showcases, advertising on their Web site, etc.).

294. You invite them to come hear you speak when you are in the area.

295. You have intelligence and a message and are funny on stage and off.

296. You have a firm fee schedule, with no add-on fees.

297. You never charge a lesser fee to any customer than the gross fee you ask the bureau to charge.

298. You refer leads from your speeches booked by a bureau back to the booking bureau.

299. You call the bureau with great leads that are ready to buy and ask the bureau to handle it, even though the bureau was not connected with the lead.

300. When a buyer books you directly, you ask if they need another speaker, then have one of your bureaus call them with ideas.

301. You ask bureaus how you can help them sell you.

302. You are an expert. A real expert.

303. You refer clients back to the bureau if they have a question or concern.

304. You refer the bureau's clients back to bureau if they call you directly.

305. You are able to tell the bureau that after every presentation, you will be sending leads from the audience, and that your average so far is ____.

306. You are able to tell the bureau, "Last year I paid out $50,000 in commissions on ancillary (product) sales to bureaus."

307. You are able to show the bureau that other speakers' bureaus are booking you, and who they are.

308. When buyers ask you, "Do we *have* to use a bureau? Can't you cut your price if you and I work together?," you never reply with, "Once a bureau or agent gets involved, I don't have any choice. I am stuck. We have to work through the bureau. If I don't, all of the other agents and bureaus will get mad at me. They know each other."

Instead, say, "My fees are always the same, if you call me or my bureau. Their tremendous service is free to you and actually a great advantage. They have several thousand speakers available on every possible topic. If something happened to me, they would have a back-up speaker there for you immediately. They chose me for you out of hundreds of possibilities because they are good at making the right match."

309.   You are the kind of person who promotes the bureau—someone who pays dividends on the time and effort a bureau invests in you.

310.   You print the bureau's name and phone number on all of your handouts, promotional materials, and giveaways for dates at which the bureau books you. Any speaker who takes the time and trouble to work with a bureau in this way makes sure that he or she is a gilt-edged investment.

311.   You remember that the speakers' bureau is your customer.

312.   You act as if the bureaus earn a commission, not as if they take a commission. You understand they gave you 75 percent of the fee; you did not give them 25 percent.

313.   You are excited to hear from the bureaus and appreciate anything they do for you.

314.   You are a genuine person with a burning desire to share your messages.

315.   You are not afraid of a little advice. You know there is room to grow and are open to learning.

316.   You ask, "How can I prove to you that you will be pleased if you book me?" and listen!

317.   You are polite and make the bureau feel they are a giant in the industry for whom you have great respect.

318. You do not have an attitude about the unfairness of the world, and speakers' bureaus in particular, when they do not book you immediately.

319. You take the time to be interested in the bureau person—not just the work, but the person. You take the time to connect with them on a personal level.

Stand out in the Crowd With Speakers' Bureaus

320. When a customer is ready to book you, instead of just handling the contract, ask the buyer to call a specific speakers' bureau instead. That really makes the bureau take notice.

321. When you have a booking in a particular city, be sure to invite local bureau representatives to come and hear you.

322. Ask the bureau to review your materials or presentation director's notes, and pay for the time. This is a great way to obtain coaching and expert advice and will certainly help you form a relationship.

323. After each presentation you do for a bureau, call and give a report. Only about 20 percent of the speakers I work with have done that, and bureaus love it when they check in.

324. Immediately give the bureau the cards of the prospects you picked up at the presentation. Ask bureaus if they would like to follow up on the leads or if you should. They all have differing policies.

325. Print up business cards in very small quantities, with your name and the bureau's name, to give out at dates for which the bureau books you.

326. Don't just say, "Thank you, I appreciate what you did for me." Send a thank-you when you get booked. A handwritten card is the most impressive.

327. If you have several bureaus working for you, impeccable record keeping is imperative. Some meeting planners call several bureaus at once and ask each bureau to make suggestions to them according to the planner's specifications. Those specifications will lead most bureaus to suggest the same speaker. Therefore many bureaus might call you about the same date and client. Keep careful records about which bureau called you first!

328. Be prepared to pay a double commission if two bureaus have done work on the same client. In the long run it will be worth the money you lose to keep both bureaus happy. It does not happen that often.

329. Be prepared to pay a commission for a date you were already working on yourself. It is better to reward the bureau for thinking of you than to lose that bureau as a potential source of income.

330. When customers call you, always ask some very gentle probing questions so you can credit the source of the lead.

331. Contact bureaus and invite them to send their clients located in the area in which you are speaking.

332. Ask yourself how you can help the account reps at speakers' bureaus earn more money and have more fun.

Rainmaking to Fill Your Income Streams

WHAT YOU NEED TO KNOW

333. Treat speaking, training, and consulting like a business. Put up-front time into learning it. By the time you become a skillful presenter with a marketable, compelling message, you won't have to spin your wheels learning how to market yourself.

334. Plan on spending at least half of your time working on marketing and selling your services.

335. Set aside time—two days a week, or part of each day—to do nothing but marketing.

336. Use the 80/20 rule: look for the few marketing things that make the most difference, then work on building those.

Don't Quit Your Day Job

337. Don't quit your day job until you have plenty of funding. You will not be able to concentrate on success if you are desperate about finances. Make the move to full time, when it doesn't matter anymore—when you are making more money with your "hobby" than your full-time job.

Get Back to Basics

338. Go over everything you do and create, and pretend you are starting over. What would you do differently?

339. Do not work on your external marketing until you become very knowledgeable about your content.

340. Do not work on your external marketing until you become skilled as a presenter.

Make a Marketing Plan

341. There are many great speakers, trainers, and consultants who are unknown because they do not know how to market themselves. Likewise, there are many mediocre speakers, trainers, and consultants speakers who are successful because they are great at marketing. Once you are adept at your speaking skills and knowledge base, work strenuously on your marketing plan.

342. Why do you need to speak? (Step 1 in your marketing plan)

343. How will people find out about you? (Step 2 in creating a marketing plan)

344. Using your computer, take 30 days and write down all of your ideas for increasing your income. Sort them, and start your plan from that.

Profiting from Paperwork

345. Paperwork is not just busy work, it is a mandatory marketing and customer service tool. Put everything you have agreed to in writing—even a letter with the details in bullets will do. Working as far out as we do makes it very easy to forget what everyone has agreed to, such as expenses for two in exchange for a lesser fee, 10 extra banquet tickets for a family that lives in the area of the event, and so forth. Putting it all in writing shows that you were listening and that you understand what the client wants of you.

346. In addition to the terms of your agreement, a contract can act as a way to bring other services you offer in front of the buyer. For example, an addendum based on your fee schedule, or a simple reference on your fee schedule, can often bring more business in the door.

347.   Offer a discount scale to entice early payment. The earlier the client pays, the larger the discount.

348.   A preprogram questionnaire takes all of the information from your contract and your discussions, and puts it into a questionnaire format. Do not have your clients fill out information they have given you in previous discussions. A simple computer program can keep fields filled in when clients give you information. Before you send the questionnaire, fill in as many blanks as you can using the information the buyer has already given you.

349.   After the engagement, in addition to your follow-up calls, send a letter asking for ideas on who might benefit from your services.

Associate with and Study Successful Experts in Your Industry

350.   If you want to be successful, study those who have achieved success. Associate with successful speakers, consultants, and trainers. Watch and learn how they market and even comport themselves.

351.   Assume you know nothing. You will learn a great deal this way!

352.   Form a mastermind group of other speakers/ consultants/trainers who are also well on their way. Have sessions once a month to share ideas. These sessions can easily be held via a group phone meeting.

Hire a Coach or Mentor

353.   If your resources allow, pay for consultations with those who have succeeded and whom you admire. There are those who claim to be consultants in this industry. Finding someone who really knows what is going on will cut years off your learning curve. Do your research. Someone else's eyes examining your work can often see a great deal more than you can.

What Makes the Greatest Presenters?

Practice

354. Get up and speak anywhere you can, whether it's Toastmasters or volunteering for small group situations. You must have places to hone your skills in a relatively risk-free and stimulating environment. You should never practice on your clients.

355. There are some things you'll never learn until you have presented your subject 500 times. Find ways to hit that magic 500 with free and fee talks.

356. Practice, practice, practice. Especially practice out loud. Make tapes and listen to them; make videos and watch them.

357. Ask for feedback. Take it seriously and do not question it.

358. Find a mentor who will give you honest feedback on your speaking skills.

359. Write out every word of your presentation. Craft it perfectly on paper. Read it out loud into an audio tape recorded in small segments. Stop and record over those segments you were not happy with. Listen to the perfect edited version of the tape over and over. Only by knowing what you want to say very well can you relax and concentrate instead on your audience. You seemed "canned" when you do not have the material firmly ingrained.

More Tips on Creating a Great Speech

360. At best, the audience will only remember 10 percent of what you say, or about three points. What three things do you want your audience to remember? Create your presentations and written materials around those three things.

361. If you want to be a great speaker, study great speakers. Go see and/or listen to tapes of the best speakers in action.

362. If you want to be funny, study humorists and comedians. Buy tapes and see live performances of those you think are funny.

Your Words Must Change Lives and Solve Problems

363. You cannot measure the success of your talk by how much you were enjoyed the day of the talk. Speaking success is measured years after the speech, by the change your words created in the actions and attitudes of the those whose lives you touched.

364. Work on the most important part of your talk, which is knowing what it is you must motivate or convince them to do. Even if you are a 100 percent comedian, getting them to laugh is your objective.

365. Be clear on the value you bring to the platform. Be very good at helping your audience solve problems and create change with your information.

Be About It, Believe It, Live It

366. You must become a person of success before you talk about being a person of success. The most popular presenters are those who are real-life examples of their message. What can you do to become a real-life example?

367. Don't discount your own successes. Each of us has overcome and accomplished. Tell your story and your personal experience. Tell of your failures and triumphs. Tell of the lessons these taught you. Then give strategies for how listeners can apply these lessons to their lives.

368. *"They call it coaching, but it is teaching. You do not tell them it is so. You show them it is so."*
—Vince Lombardi, Sr.

369. Be a person who not only talks about but shows us honesty, character, and sincerity. Your sincerity will shine through when you speak from your passion—from your heart. The audience must believe that you believe. And they will believe you, if you believe you.

370. *"Though an able speaker charms me with his eloquence, I say, I'd rather see a sermon than to hear, any day."*
—Edgar A. Guest

Study the Superstars, but Be Unique

371. Study everyone; imitate no one.

372. Do not go where the path may lead, but go where there is no path, and leave a trail. Differentiate yourself from all other speakers. What you are, what you do, and what you speak need to combine into a uniqueness. Take time to define and/or become a unique expert.

373. Having consequential wisdom to give your listeners is vital, but you will only make it in this industry if you are creative in how you present that wisdom.

374. Evaluate opportunities to present before you accept, to see if they are a fit with your unique message. Never compromise your message.

THE BASICS OF RAINMAKING

The Expert and Leading Authority: The Highest Paid of All!

375. To be successful as a presenter, the information you present must be not only well delivered but specialized. Brain surgeons earn 10 times the salary of a general practitioner—it pays to be an expert.

376. What is your single area of expertise that is your greatest strength? Find ways to vividly and credibly characterize what your area of expertise is based on your actual experience. Be exceedingly clear on what your strengths are and what messages and expertise you have. No one will buy your service if *you* don't know what you're selling!

377. Study and research constantly. As you study and restudy your topic, you will gain perspective on the material that is uniquely your own. Immersing yourself in your subject allows you to speak with power. As Benjamin Disraeli said, "Eloquence is the child of knowledge."

378.   Do not stray from your areas of core competency unless you become an expert in a new topic or niche. This will happen as you study and research each new industry you work with to discover its unique needs.

Where Paid Experts Find Knowledge

379.   Search out all the ways to find facts and insights for your target market: the library, the Internet, used book stores, industry publications, e-zines, e-news, industry association Web sites, and more. Look for ways to gather knowledge that others do not commonly pursue.

380.   Continue going to seminars and lectures regularly to hear what other speakers on your subject have to say and how they say it. You must know more than these people and speak better than they do. Buy their books and other products as well.

381.   If you use or adapt other speakers' material, give them credit. You will lose income if people stop using your services because they note you are just a copycat.

382.   Offer to assist a great presenter on your topic when he or she comes to your area. Assisting another expert is one of the best ways to gather knowledge about the good (and bad) ways to do things. Do not offer to help, then take up time talking about you! Honestly find ways to help as best you can.

Search in Every Niche and Cranny

383.   Spend time at the front end of your career soul-searching for the answer to the question, "Who can I best serve?" Now you know which target to focus on your positioning.

384.   Target a small specific market. You can be a general practitioner type of presenter if you have targeted a smaller specific market. Instead of saying your target market is "anyone who might use a presenter in the entire universe," you target a specific group in which to be the expert. Then your very common type of topic becomes much in demand. In this world it is much better to be a big fish in a small pond.

385. Focus your marketing efforts on those companies and industries that can *afford to pay* for your services.

386. Find a niche that is unique.

387. Once you have prospective niches, explores what niche-within-a-niche markets would be most interested on your topics as presented by you.

388. Focus what you do into one sentence. If you cannot tell the world what you do in just a few words, you are not yet ready to venture forth.

Become a Celebrity in a Small Pond: Branding

389. Brand yourself with a specialty. Became a celebrity in the market that uses that specialty.

390. In all of your materials, decide on what you want branded with your name. It is your company name? The Smith Group? When someone has a need to fill, they will not be thinking of the Smith solution. But they might be thinking of "The Cold Call Specialist," or "Experts on Internet Issues." These are concepts you want branded with your name and company. Include them with everything you create: business cards, letterheads, products.

Start with Your Own

391. Target the markets from which you have sprung. Your own background, business experience, or perhaps military experience, and youth leadership such as the Boy Scouts or Girl Scouts, family, or education (either in the academic or business world). These are the foundation on which you can easily stand as a speaker, trainer, or consultant.

392.   If your background market is one that has no money, then find out who is already selling things to that market and start with them.

Does Anyone Like You? Sidelong Looks

393.   Market to your best bets first—those you are fairly sure will buy.

394.   Look at what business you are already getting, then look laterally. Once you are successful with your topic in one market, customize it to suit a related group. That sales association you spoke for can supply you with a list of other chapters of the same association. The branch of the bank where you performed has a list of its branches and of financial associations they belong to.

395.   Market to all of the suppliers to the industry you currently are working in.

396.   Market to all of those that the industry you are currently working in is supplying with its products or services.

How to Get Lateral Marketing Business

397.   Ask for a letter of recommendation from the initial group. This letter will open doors to related groups.

398.   Call first, then send a letter of inquiry to the new group, mentioning the names of the key people in the first group, with copies of your letters of recommendation.

399.   Your promotional package of materials should be customized to show you are an expert in this new industry. Literature and letters of recommendation from your past buyers should show you as an expert on your topic, but mention the industries related to the new group.

400.   Compile some of the best comments from the rating sheets from companies in related or sister industries. Include these in your materials to new, related industries.

401. Market to industries whose interests are linked with those of the associations or businesses for which you have already worked. For example, if your first successes are in banking, then try savings and loans, escrow companies, credit associations, and real estate brokers, which might lead to building contractors and plumbers.

Ways that Work While You're Out Working

402. There is no such thing as true passive marketing. Passive marketing takes up-front work to set it in place and maintenance along the way. But you can and should aim to put something in place that has a generous payoff with a minimal amount of effort.

403. The most popular and effective form of passive marketing strategy is exposure through your writing, articles, and the press.

404. Write monthly columns for newspaper, newsletters, magazines, e-zines, or Web sites.

405. Create products with your contact information. A good product will be solid over time, bringing you leads years from now. Your products should always talk about you in your other roles: speaker, consultant, coach, and so on.

406. Send your products to everyone who might do a review and/or interview. Call first!

407. Provide reprints of articles on subjects that interest your customers as a free gift (with your contact information).

408. Create a business-size card with the three or five main points that you want clients to remember, also with your contact information. Give these cards out at your talks. Encourage clients to go over the points several times a week. A card they keep in their wallet because of how it helps them will ensure they never forget how to reach you.

409. Do a newsletter weekly, monthly, or at least quarterly, filled with great information and a tiny smattering of promotion on yourself, and a review of one of your products. This can be sent out via mail, fax, or e-mail. It can be a free promotion or subscription-based.

410. Create giveaways with your contact info (keychains, pens) that you know clients will continue to use. Items that are *useful* are kept.

411. Create a giveaway with a quote you are famous for. Have this quote printed on coffee mugs, tee shirts, notepads, and so on. Include your contact number very discreetly on the product.

412. Make your handouts so valuable and reusable that they will be keepers. Your contact information will be on each page. Design them in ways that make them easily accessible next to their desk.

413. Develop a cooperative marketing group of three or four other professionals in complementary but not competitive areas. Share leads and recommend each other for groups you have already spoken to.

414. Include speakers' bureau representatives on your mailing lists, newsletter lists, marketing lists, and gift lists.

415. Hire a pleasant, helpful, happy person to answer the telephone and to market you.

416. Make sure your staff experiences the excitement of being in your audience.

417. Hire a public relations person to work on getting your materials into the press.

418. Provide your clients with a menu of circumstances. They might not be aware of all of the types of events at which your programs would work.

419. When you join e-mail discussion groups, make sure to include a link to your Web site in your signature.

These messages are posted at Web sites and are often forwarded on. Every link to you on the Web helps your ratings in the search engines.

420.   Sign your e-mail! E-mail automatically tells the receiver the e-mail address of the sender; however "SweetiePie@aol.com" is not very informative in a business communication. Also, when you print the e-mail onto your printer, it might not even give the address. Most e-mail programs have a way to add your signature to every piece of e-mail. This can include anything you want: your name, phone, Web address, new product release, upcoming seminar dates, and so on.

Books and Products

421.   Books work for you while you are working for your clients. Creating a book may be your single most important passive marketing tool. All of your other products will begin to sell better when you have a book out there promoting them.

422.   With just a limited number of days to speak (100 max), products are the best way to grow your business. Create them, then learn to sell them!

423.   Quote colleagues and the bureaus who book you in the books you write and in your other products. It builds relationships and encourages them to work for you.

424.   Collaborate with other industry leaders to coauthor books—even if it means you do most of the work.

425.   Read Chap. 4.

Articles and Newsletters

426.   Articles work for you while you are working for your clients.

427.   Quote colleagues and the bureaus who book you in the articles you write. It builds relationships and encourages them to work for you.

428.   Your free newsletter can be your least expensive and most effective marketing tool.

Speakers' Bureaus

429.   Speakers' bureaus can be your number one source of passive bookings. Read the section "Agents, Speakers' Bureaus, and Middlemen" in Chap. 2.

More and More Income-Increasing Tips and Strategies

430.   Add to your fee schedule that your program is also available for groups in various sizes. List each size as a separate item on your fee schedule, especially if you are including training materials in the fee, in which case you can offer to give a price break when the number of attendees increases.

Customization: Profit by Uncovering, Targeting, and Meeting Needs

431.   A highly customized program is worth more than a simply personalized program.

432.   Personalize your program by contacting a portion or all of the attendees. Add their comments and quotes throughout your written and oral materials.

433.   Do a survey of all of the upcoming attendees, then use the survey results throughout your presentation to the group. This is a real selling point!

434.   Find ways to show in your marketing materials that your presentation really is going to be highly customized. Simply saying that what you do is customized is not enough.

435.   Keep careful records of survey results from all former presentations. Do a yearly report compiling all of the results for each specific industry. In each new report, compare results from the previous years. Use all results anonymously! This customized report can be sold as a separate product or as an add-on benefit.

436.   Send a preprogram questionnaire to the key officials. In addition to being a great marketing tool, it enables you to do some terrific customization.

437.   Go to your customers' Internet sites and read their press releases. Here you will see what your customers perceive as important.

Offer Your Programs in Less Time with More Value

438.   Shorter sessions that offer solutions to your clients' challenges in less time are very valuable. The key is to find ways to deliver the information that will also change their actions and their attitudes, but in less time.

439.   Try a modularized training design that requires minimum time off the job and/or during off-peak work times with follow-up on-the-job programs offered in modules.

440.   Offer a program with backup products and training materials which can be used on the job to learn while working.

441.   Find ways to deliver your specific information while people are on the job, perhaps via telephone.

442.   Offer one-on-one personal onsite coaching while people are actually on the job.

Making a Profit in Your Own Land

443.   You are a good investment for meetings coming to your hometown, because they can save air fare and hotel bills if they use you. Target your marketing efforts to those groups coming to your hometown.

444.   Work up an additional talk about your own area. Cover local history, customers, shopping opportunities, or other area-specific topics. This can be a great add-on to your other programs. Event planners often use these programs especially for spouse programs.

445. Send meeting planners who are coming into your area a small newsletter with news of your community and your topic. Offer to be of service and help in advance. Repeat the fact that by using you, they can save hotel bills and airfare.

446. Join and become involved with your local convention and visitors' bureau. Bureaus know and sell information on which groups are coming to your area.

447. Build relationships with local venue staff working with incoming meetings. A local interest speaker would be someone they would talk about to their clients.

448. Join and become involved with your local service clubs, which often have as members who are executives from large businesses in your area.

449. Make sure your press and publicity efforts target the concerns of businesses in your area.

How to Add New Programs and Services

450. Evolve your keynotes into training.

451. Evolve your training into keynotes.

452. Evolve from seminars a few hours long to multiple-day engagements including research, writing, and presentations.

453. Contact your old customers yearly to find out what their new needs are. This will tell you what you need to research for new programs.

454. Add the information you gather from your yearly getting-in-touch calls to your reports and other products. References to actual companies should be anonymous—do not mention the specific companies or give coy clues as to who they might be.

455. Use the information you gather in your yearly getting-in-touch calls to create new programs.

456. Make sure all of those additional opportunities are listed on your fee schedule.

Distributors

457. Train, certify, and assign distributorships or even franchises to other people who will present your programs and sell your materials. Sell the use of your program and/or products to those who are good speakers but bad researchers. Once your program is proven before many audiences and starts to be in demand in the marketplace, you will be ready to look for distributors. Allowing others to sell your products and ideas increases your income and visibility in an ever widening geographic range, and multiplies the opportunities to help others.

458. The best potential distributors for your programs can be found in your seminars. Those who like the subject and are enthusiastic about your personality are the ones to invite to become distributors.

Train Your Current Customers' Distributors

459. Go to companies that are compatible with your area of expertise. Suggest the client hire you to go out and train the distributors and retailers who sell their products. You might make a career out of this one sponsor.

460. Offer a specific company exclusivity for a limited period of time. When the contract expires, offer this type of training to the company's competitors.

461. Go laterally to those in similar industries.

462. Develop contracts with companies to outsource their training on a scheduled basis.

Just Smart Business

463. Save and invest some of your income; have a cash reserve before you give up your day job.

464. Put 20 percent of everything you make in term deposits to see you through the inevitable slow periods.

465. Eliminate time consumers that do not produce. Concentrate on the 20 percent of your efforts that do work for you.

466.   Market to those who buy everything you sell in the arena where you have credibility.

467.   Work first on regional and state conferences in order to book national conferences.

468.   Contact all local meeting planners and speakers' bureaus whenever you are performing in a city in which you speak. Not only can you invite them to see you speak—with permission of your customer—but you might just do an office visit, with a short in-person survey as the reason for your visit.

469.   Do at least five actions a day that will move your success forward. Maybe these are calls, faxes, or e-mails. Whatever they are, they add up.

470.   Set yourself a goal to close a deal a day. This might be small promotion, an article, or a book sale. But confirm one a day.

471.   Set goals. Goals are dreams with a deadline. Put them up where everyone in your office can see them and make every bit of work you do propel you toward them. When you reach those goals, aim for new ones immediately.

472.   Don't let up on your marketing efforts or you will pay the price.

PROMOTIONAL STRATEGIES

Most people think promotion is just something to do with advertising. But it is so much more.

473.   Think promotion in every single thing you do. It begins with your own business cards, stationery, envelopes, and labels, and extends to your personal appearance. Perhaps the best promotion is the aura of excellence you convey in your service to your customers, from the way you answer the telephone to the speed with which you return a phone call and the personal thank-you notes for every referral and every person who helps you or books you.

474.   Celebrity experts are able to command much higher fees than the average expert. The greater your celebrity status, the less effective you need to be as a speaker! The world is willing to pay to be in the same room with a celebrity. To be fair, the better the celebrity is at speaking, the higher the fees he or she is able to obtain. Once clients recognize your name, your fees will increase dramatically. Becoming famous will not happen by itself. The articles you read and the stories you see and hear in the media do not appear there by accident. Think promotion!

Raving Fan Relationships: One-on-One Marketing

475.   Do more one-on-one marketing. In our age of impersonal contact, overwhelming bulk e-mails and scripted telemarketers, one-on-one is golden. Develop relationships with clients and prospects.

476.   Do such a good job in all levels of contact with your buyers that you create in them raving fans. Then, those who give you referrals will actively speak on your behalf. Once they are talking about you in an enthusiastic way, the rest is easy.

477.   It's not what you know, it's who you know. You can be a brilliant speaker, but if you cannot form relationships with the meeting planners, event planners, and speakers' bureaus that will book you, it will be like trying to row upstream without a paddle.

478.   Find out your customers' birthdays and mail them cards. Everyone mails holiday cards. Try for the more personal approach.

479.   Take responsibility for achieving the customer's objectives.

480.   Add all of your contacts into a database, with personal notes about them. Keep in touch with all these people every 90 days.

481. .   Watch for interviews, articles, and mentions of companies and clients in your field of expertise. Clip out the articles and send them to the company in the story. Attach a note of congratulations. Tell them how much the article helped you.

482.   Keep in touch through e-mails, newsletters, and articles, but remember that personal contact is the most valuable of all. An occasional phone call is golden and a handwritten note is the best of all.

Do You Really Know Who They Are?

483.   Know your customers! Know their industry and their company.

484.   Know a little bit about the people with whom you are in direct contact. Get to know them as people. *Public relations* literally means your relationships with other people. The way to find friends is to be friends.

485.   Customers are impressed and flattered when you remember what they have told you. Write down ideas they share with you. It is a great way to bond with customers and team members (not to mention it acts as a great way to ensure that you remember to do what you say you will do!).

Find Ways to Say Thank You

486.   Actively showing appreciation raises value. It is hard to forget someone who often gives real appreciation.

487.   When you are on the road, there is that endless wait at the airport or the time on board the flight. Use those times constructively by catching up on your thank-yous via your laptop computer, e-mail, and faxes, or carry your customized postcards and send a personal note to those who have interviewed you, booked you, or helped you.

Giving Gifts and Bribes

488.   There is a fine line between a well received, thoughtful gift and one that is perceived as a bribe. Send gifts to specific customers for specific reasons. These should be inexpensive but very appropriate to that person, or their company. For a person who told you she is wild about gardens, you might send a vintage book on gardening from eBay. Other appropriate ideas might be a travel brochure or an article from a magazine about a place a customer told you he wished he could go, a few pieces of her favorite candy, or a card with a picture of the same type of dog he said he has. Most things you or a family member create are almost always appropriate.

489. When you send a gift, make sure it says why you are sending it. Be specific.

490. Gifts that can be shared with staff are always well received.

491. Gifts to customers should never be crude or off-color.

Gifts that Stay on Their Desks

492. Look around your office and note the useful items that stay on your desks. Useful items will be kept. These might be . . .

493. Sticky note pads (perhaps with your name and address). I got one shaped like Mickey Mouse from the Disneyland Pacific Hotel! The first few notes had opportunity dates on which the hotel offers group discounts marked on a calendar.

494. Pens with yellow highlighters on them (some have a pen and highlighter in the same pen). These stay with users until they run dry.

495. An elegant, high-quality pen engraved with your name and the client's.

Off-the-Platform Superstars

496. When you step on the speaking platform, you step into a fishbowl. You will be judged not only as the person you show to the world on stage and in print, but perhaps even more so as the person you are behind the scenes. Once you decide to take the platform, even for small companies or free speeches, every move you make on stage and off is talked about and scrutinized.

497.   Once you are at the lectern speaking, you are the star. But in the minutes and hours before your appearance, as well as afterward, you should think of yourself as their helper. If something needs to be done, (i.e., chairs moved, copies made, etc.), just go do it yourself—with a smile.

498.   On and off the platform, be pleasant to work with, flexible, and cooperative. Do not argue with anyone. You would be amazed at how many speakers are not called because they have a reputation of being cranky and difficult.

499.   Think of everything that should be taken care of. Create a checklist of all of these things, and handle what you can yourself. You want the client to rave afterwards, "You thought of everything!" See the bonus checklist in Chap. 5.

500.   Send a thank-you to your customers and anyone that helped you during your presentation. In this day of rapid-fire e-mail, faxes, and phones, a handwritten note and a card mean a great deal. Yes, I've mentioned this many times—it's that important!

501.   Be delighted with other people's success. Show it. Send appreciative comments. Mean it.

Ways to Keep Your Name Current

Tracking Leads

502.   One of the most important aspects of marketing is tracking how you are getting your leads and when to follow up with them. In fact, if you don't develop a system for tracking, you will not be in business long. A contact management system will help you establish which of your advertising, direct mail, and publicity projects are the most effective and should be repeated. This is most easily done with a database run from your computer, but even 3×5 index cards will work.

503.   Never fail to fill out the field in tracking software for every incoming call which tells you where and how this business is coming in the door. You will only know the answer to this question if you ask.

504. You must work your tracking system. It not enough to simply track the leads; you must work the leads.

505. Have a follow-up timing system, so you know when customers would like you to call them back.

506. It is imperative that you track incoming inquiries not only for your own benefit, but also to maximize the use of multiple nonexclusive bureaus that obtain bookings for you. If the caller heard you at a program, ask which program. Check your records. How was that program booked? If it was booked for you by a bureau, get all the information first, then call the lead to your bureau. The bureau will appreciate your honesty about the client and will work for you enthusiastically on new bookings. If the lead came from a fellow speaker or business client, send out a thank-you letter the same day.

Speaking Calendars

507. Mail your abbreviated calendar (possibly included as part of a newsletter and/or e-news) to your past and future buyers. List your clients and location on the calendar. Seeing that you are really out there working for major clients is an excellent way to promote bookings. Success breeds success.

508. Always include your topics and your personal name on your calendar. "The 21 Century Group" is not enough. It is your unique and interesting topics and/or specialty that you want customers to associate with you.

Free Promotional Newsletters

509. Keep your name current with newsletters. Newsletters can be sent via mail, fax, or e-mail. The best are filled with quick, fast, interesting tips that clients can use in business today. This sort of newsletter is more apt to be copied and passed around (which is exactly what you hope will happen).

510.   Your newsletter must include your name, a brief mention of your topics, and how to reach you.

511.   Electronic newsletters (newsletters sent out via e-mail) are almost free to send, immediate, and so easy a child can send them. Maintaining your list can be a hassle, unless you use a listserv, which does cost a small fee.

512.   Include in your newsletter things like:

- Interesting news; useful, practical tips; announcements; and specials.

- Ask a question and combine the most interesting responses into one lengthy message.

- Polls of the most useful books your readership thinks have helped them, and poll results.

- Survey results, which you can gather via your newsletter.

Promotional Systems and Ideas

The Magic Is in the Mix

513.   Your name must be seen, and seen again, at least five times to finally sink in.

514.   Calling five times just turns people off of using you—permanently. But there are many other ways to put your name in front of people. The magic is in the mixing of all promotional, publicity, advertising ideas, and phone calls.

515.   Since advertising is often expensive, consider sharing promotion and advertising with other speakers in complementary but not competing fields. Team up to buy a joint ad or Web site. An extra advantage to the teaming arrangement can be the shared use of a toll-free, wide-area 800 number. You might even jointly hire a staff person to answer the phones and send out promotional materials.

Leave a Trail that Leads Back to You

516.   Always leave a trail that leads back to your headquarters or to your speakers' bureau. Make sure that nothing goes out that does not lead back to you.

517.   Your handouts and workbooks should have your name and phone number clearly on each page (if you were booked through a bureau, make sure to put its name on each page).

518.   Give a small gift to all participants in your sessions. This is a gift that they will not throw away that contains your name and phone number.

519.   Have some of your short essays, poems, posters, or articles printed or decoupaged on plaques or reproduced on fine-quality paper stock suitable for framing. This way people who receive such a gift will want to hang it on their wall. Of course, it needs to say, "A Special Gift from _____," with your contact information. Remember a sheet of paper costs a fraction of a cent. It is the idea printed on it that has unlimited value and potential.

520.   Add a box to the bottom of your articles, or mention as part of the verbal interview, a freebie people will get if they call you. In an article on "The Speaker Expense Dilemma" which I wrote for a major meeting planner magazine, I included a closing box that said: "To obtain a free copy of the Walters International Speakers Bureau form for speaker expenses, call Lilly Walters, 909-398-1228." I received over 300 requests from prospective buyers. The giveaway was only a piece of paper, but an invaluable piece of information that helped solve a problem for meeting planners.

521.   Begin thinking of a survey you can take, or a series of articles, or lists you can compile based on your subject such as the "Ten Rules," "Eight Tips," or "Five Little-Known Secrets." Make every word valuable to the audience you want to reach.

522.   In all of your promotional articles and interviews, be sure to drop the hint that you are *the* expert on this subject, with so much more to tell . . . if only there was time. Be warned that this works only if you give such tremendous information and insights that customers are eager to hear more. Leave them unsatisfied and this becomes a sure method of getting yourself staring at a phone that is not ringing.

Direct Mail

523.　Direct mail refers to sending out promotional material to mass mailing lists you have gathered or rented. Remember, direct mail produces about 1 percent return at best, so expect approximately 50 inquiries from a 5000-piece mailing. When you follow up those 50 leads, you can expect to close about 10 bookings, providing you had good copy and mailed to the right prospects.

524.　Do not mail your full package of promotional materials out via direct mail! It is terribly expensive and a waste of time.

525.　Do direct mail of a single inquiry letter or postcard.

526.　Do regular mailings to your own mailing list.

527.　Do repeated mailings once every two months. Send interesting and short bits of information on your topics.

528.　Create "Lumpy letters." These get opened, and people remember you and the contents.

Directories

529.　List yourself in directories that meeting planners use. All the major associations that cater to those that hire speakers (MPI, ASAE, PCMA, etc.) have directories in which they sell space.

530.　Regional as well as national directories of speakers are published and carried on the World Wide Web. Some require membership in their group before a speaker is listed, while others sell listings and display advertising space to any speaker who will pay. Many are free.

531.　Use the major search engines on the Web, and look for directories or yellow pages. Also search under your topic area and see if someone is developing a directory of experts in your area of expertise.

532.　Several radio and television talent directories are published and can list you and your area of expertise. These directories often are used by radio and television stations when they need someone to interview on a particular topic. Most have an advertising fee.

More Ways to Boost Income with Advertising

533.   Use targeted advertising media. You will get a greater return on your investment.

534.   Whenever you advertise anywhere and receive any results, it's a good thing. Make it much better by getting some free advertising in return. Call clients and ask if they use testimonials in any of their materials. Offer to give them one. These are published and work to promote you as they give testimony.

535.   Call the same the groups you advertise with (not on the Internet), and ask for the Web designer. Suggest that you would like to do a testimonial for them to include on their Web site. This is often handled by a different person than the one who handles hard-copy testimonials.

Barter for Advertising

536.   It can be beneficial to your career to exchange your speaking fee for advertising space or time. In return for performing, you are able to advertise your services as a speaker or promote your seminars and products in the client's publications or media.

537.   Certain publications and radio stations pay for articles or training, while some wish they could but don't have the funds. In this case suggest a barter or an advertising exchange—your products or services for an ad(s).

538.   Barter with those groups for which you are currently speaking. If these groups will not buy your product themselves in bulk before an event, try negotiating an ad in the some of the literature. You might offer to do an additional spouse program for them at no fee in exchange for ads. Most meetings have all kinds of pre, during, and post literature, newsletters, and brochures which the groups produce. It costs nothing to put an ad in them.

539.   There are trade shows of all kinds and sizes aimed at every market. Many trade shows look for professional speakers who will trade a presentation aimed at their particular group for a free booth and/or a display ad in the trade show program or directory. This is a good bargain. You have the opportunity to speak to an ideal audience of prospects and to sell your speaking services and products at a booth.

Speaking Engagements as Promotion Opportunities

540.   Wherever you speak, invite people to come and hear you—editors, producers, bureau representatives, potential clients. Inviting people to preview you is an excellent promotional strategy. Call ahead and make arrangements.

541.   There is no better promotion for your speaking career than being very good on and off the platform!

542.   At every presentation, always think of a way to do more than you are asked to do. In addition to going more than the extra mile in preparing and giving the presentation, be cheerful and helpful off the platform.

CULTIVATING SALES, REPEATS, SPIN-OFFS, AND REFERRALS

543.   Since most people belong to several organizations and associations, they can and will provide many contacts if you cultivate them.

Getting Booked a Second Time

544.   Anyone can get booked once. Long-term success depends on giving value as promised for scarce educational dollars. Survival depends on delivering benefits rather than hype.

Ask for Referrals

545.   Ask those in your database to look at their immediate circle of influence. Ask if they can think of those who might benefit from what you do. Ask if they would introduce you to them.

546. Train your customers to sell you! Discuss with your current customers gentle ways they could talk to other people, to explain their experience with you. Do not send them into the fray without some suggestions on what to say. Do not suggest that they say you are great, great, great. Instead, go over the benefits that you remember and are tracking in your database from the presentations you did for them.

547. The best, most constant, and least expensive source of new bookings is your most recent audience.

548. Find ways to collect the business cards of those in the audience who are holding events, such as drawings, or turn in worksheets.

549. Have a system set up as part of your presentation that allows you to help attendees in the learning process, but also gives you a way to subtly ask for referrals, such as:

- Follow-up e-mails, or turning in long-term homework.

- Follow-up phone calls to check their progress, or turning in long-term homework.

- Follow-up letters to check their progress, or turning in long-term homework.

550. In the Q&A, make sure you say, "If you are interested in my doing a program like this for you, just give me your business cards and write on the back the date of the event at which you want me to speak."

Creating New Engagements from the Present One

Ways of Expanding the Booking

551. When clients call to book you for one session at a conference or convention, ask, "What other types of speakers are you still trying to find for this event?" Offer to do the extra program for them at a reduced rate. They will save on fees, airfare, and hotel accommodations.

552. Have all of the services you offer shown on your fee schedule!

553. Always ask your current customers if they are planning other upcoming events. Discuss their needs and objectives for these events. You might find a fit.

554. If you are not appropriate for your current customers' upcoming events, suggest your favorite speakers' bureaus. This will keep you in the minds of those bureaus, as well as help customers.

555. If you are not appropriate for your current customers' events, suggest another speaker with an appropriate topic. Speakers will be very inclined to return the favor when the opportune moment comes.

556. Have a multiple booking price on your fee schedule for multiple bookings contracted and deposits paid all at the same time.

Finding Spin-off Income in Your Audience

557. The very best way to find spin-off in your audience is to be so good at your craft, with such valuable knowledge, that audience members will want more.

558. Always focus first on the value of what you offer clients. If your first focus is on finding spin-offs, you cannot possibly give great value.

559. Include your calendar as a single-page handout slipped into your printed handout materials. Include the topic and industry type. This shows your expertise and market appropriateness.

560. Show on your schedule the times you have available for private career consulting sessions. You can expand your consulting and coaching business this way.

561. Paint your own professional image—otherwise the audience may assume that you have been asked to speak this one time just for fun. In the body of your program, plant the thought that you are a professional and would be a delightful and valuable speaker for other groups.

562.   Include references in your introduction that you speak on other topics.

563.   In your written introduction and closer, close with the words "[your name] has graciously agreed to stay after the program today to speak to those of you who are searching for a speaker for a future event. Now help me welcome [your name] from [your hometown or company]."

564.   Use references in your talk about other audiences, such as, "As I was on my way to speak in Chicago," or "Great question. Just last week in Los Angeles I told an audience that ____." This plants the thought that you are a professional speaker who is in demand.

565.   Always refer to yourself as a professional speaker, trainer, consultant, or whatever your focus is.

566.   Your business cards, letterhead, envelopes, and everything you print should feature your title as the "[your field] expert" and "professional speaker, trainer, and consultant."

567.   Do something in your presentation that people would love to take home—for example, recite a poem or give 10 rules of. Do not include this in your handouts. Ask the audience members if they would like a free copy. Instruct them to pull out their business cards and pass them to the person on the aisles, and your assistants will pick them up. Explain that you will mail a copy of the quote or poem to each person as a gift. Then say "Oh, while you have your card in your hand, if you are looking for a speaker/seminar leader for a future date, please just put a big S on your card."

Rating Sheets to Increase Bookings

568.   It is possible to obtain spin-off income from the present engagement using rating sheets. Use rating sheets that ask who attendees know who might enjoy a professional speaker on this same topic. (See more on this under "Ways Rating Sheets Can Help You Get

New Bookings" in Chapter 4, "Free to Shining Fee," of *Speak and Grow Rich* by Lilly and Dottie Walters.)

569.   If you do have a product table, consider printing a product order form on the back of the rating sheet. This gives them two reasons to get the paper back to you. You can modify this idea to fit your own situation. Make sure you allow plenty of time for this before the session is over.

570.   After the break, pick up the feedback sheets and stand in the traffic pattern by the coffee and refreshment area to read them.

571.   When the meeting is over, sit down with the meeting planner and review the feedback sheet results together. Especially go over the things the audience wanted to know more about. Planners usually only hear from the 2 percent of the audience that is always critical.

572.   When you get back to your office, copy the feedback sheets and send a set to the meeting planner along with a proposal to speak on another topic.

573.   Don't bother with a number scale rating sheet. A 10 rating depends too much on each listener's mood and personal belief system. Instead, create a rating sheet that asks the real questions you want answers to, such as the following points:

- What basic message did you hear that you could use tomorrow? (Purpose)

- How will you use what you heard to increase your profits and/or productivity? (Practical application)

- Is there something else about my subject that you would like to know that I did not have time to touch on in this presentation? (New topics)

- Do you know of others (businesses, associations, etc.) that would benefit from the material presented today? Who are they? (Referrals)

- What is your opinion of my presentation? (Testimonials—make sure there is a permission check box so you can use the comments.)

Rewards and Gifts
for Referrers

574. Reward referrals: Think about ways you can reward people who give you not just booked business, but also referrals. These should be small, thoughtful ways that will be greeted with appreciation, not items so expensive or large as to make the recipients feel uncomfortable.

575. Offer a finder's fee for booked dates; tell everyone you would love to pay them!

576. Put a note on your handouts, or a card on seats, of audience members, offering free gift for referrals to someone who hires—for example, free attendance at a high-end public seminar you offer, a product of yours, or a finder's fee.

Marketing Strategies
for Keeping in Touch

577. Go back to old clients before you mass-mail for new ones. Things change. Be there with a program that fits clients' current needs. Knowing what has changed with prior customers will help you create a much more effective campaign for new customers.

578. Continue contact at least twice a year.

579. Use a contact manager or database to follow up with the client during decision-making times.

580. Accumulate a list of your fans' e-mail addresses and maintain contact with them with an e-newsletter.

581. Keep in touch with past clients even if you feel they will never book you again. Remember, they all have friends and business associates.

582. Call for a reason—a book idea, a reference, a referral, and so on.

583. Find ways that are personal to keep in touch: e-mail and bulk mail are not personal.

584. Many people send Christmas cards. Try instead sending Thanksgiving, Valentine's Day, or Presidents Day messages.

585.   The best card to send to stay in touch is a birthday card.

586.   Take addresses with you when you go on trips and send postcards to your customers from the area in which you are speaking. A postcard of a local landmark is a personal touch that they will take the time to read.

Sharing and Networking to Gain Referrals

587.   You likely belong to associations, groups, or a church. Talk to the people you meet there and tell them what you do. They may be the doorway to the best series of engagements you have ever had.

588.   Give referrals to others. Give and you shall receive! Help others make connections to various meeting planners/decision makers, and help other speakers to make connections with various bureaus that would be a good mutual fit. Refer business to other speakers and bureaus. It will come back to you.

589.   After any speech, free or fee, send a thank-you note to those who allowed you to speak for them, and ask again for referrals. Help them think of where those people might be. Ask them what clubs and associations they belong to.

590.   Always say thank you to the referring person the very day you get the referral.

591.   Post information articles on your Web page and allow people to reprint them in their trade publications and company newsletters. This is a way of spreading your name and credibility.

592.   Send out articles you write to your list suggesting they use the articles whenever they would like, if they include your hyperlink and contact info.

593.   Give plugs in your newsletter to others in exchange for them giving a plug to you.

594.   Cultivate mutually beneficial relationships with people in the business world.

595. Be remembered for providing a higher-quality presentation with more take-home value than any previous speaker.

596. Ask another person to introduce you to the potential client, whether it be in person or via e-mail, phone, or snail mail.

597. Strike while the iron is hot—right after you get hired, ask immediately.

598. Don't wait! Right after a highly successful presentation, debrief every client and ask for and use referral letters.

599. When people come up after the presentation and say, "Wow, I wish you could talk to my boss/employees, or whatever," don't just leave the compliment there and expect them to follow up. Say, "Help me. . . . What do I have to do to do that?"

600. When members of the audience come up to you with praise, tell them you are interested in speaking for their company or organization. Ask them if they could help make that happen. Ask if the person you need to talk to is close by, or ask them to call the appropriate person on your cell phone right then.

601. Add a P.S. to your thank-you notes to those who have hired you, asking for a referral.

602. Target niche markets; referrals come in when you become known in a market.

603. Constantly plant seeds that you value referrals from everyone!

Special Tips for Creating Repeat Business

604. Make it clear that there is more to be said on your topic. Give as much information as you can in the time allotted to you, whether your program is a condensed version or the expanded one. It never hurts to glance at your watch and say regretfully, "I wish we had more time to go further into this point, but we don't. However, I would love to come back and work with you again!"

605. Let your audiences know that you also speak on other topics. Audience members may not consider you for another presentation if they do not realize that you have more topics to offer. Try saying something like this: "Just last week that question came up in my seminar on ____. Here is an idea I gave them. . . ."

606. Keep careful notes of each speech's content so that you can avoid repeating yourself in encore sessions. When you are booked again, your return speech must give as much honest new substance for the money as you gave the first time, and preferably more.

607. Show that you enjoyed being with the attendees and can't wait to come back. When you honestly enjoy them, they will honestly enjoy you and want you back.

608. Send buyers news about their industry.

Joining Associations that Are Best for Bookings

609. Study your target industries by joining and participating in conferences, workshops, and other events. This will be one of your best sources of leads and of gaining knowledge.

610. Join and participate in the industry association associated with your skill (either for speakers, trainers, or consultants). If finances are an issue, get involved with a local chapter even if you cannot join at the national level. Your learning curve about this business will skyrocket as you learn from people who have been where you are. Only by becoming involved will you benefit. Some possible organizations are:

611. Meeting Professionals International (MPI). Learn about what current challenges event planners face. They have speaker showcases.

612. Chamber of commerce. A meeting of local businesspeople. Chamber members can be a good source of networking. Regional and national organizations hire speakers.

613. American Society of Training and Development (ASTD). Those skilled in training meet here to learn and share. Become involved and share leads.

614. American Society of Association Executives (ASAE). Meets regionally and nationally. Speaking to associations creates wonderful opportunities to meet corporate buyers who attend.

615. Convention and visitors' bureaus. There is one in each major town. They will know which meetings are coming to town and can be a tremendous source of leads.

616. Toastmasters. A group dedicated to helping with communication confidence. It is a great place to obtain feedback on your talks. There are thousands of chapters. Some are dedicated to assisting Toastmasters to become paid public speakers. Many corporations have chapters. Members of these can be great sources of networking to obtain leads for speaking engagements within those companies.

617. National Speakers Association (NSA). Professional speakers meet regionally and nationally to learn and network. Fifty percent of those I surveyed said NSA was the number one reason for their success.

618. Society of Human Resource Management (SHRM). Many members of SHRM are responsible for bringing in outside speakers and trainers.

619. American Business Women's Association (ABWA). They are very good about helping each other and passing on leads.

620. Hospitality and Sales Marketing Association (HSMAI). Not only do they hire trainers and keynoters, but the members are all in the position to know who is looking for speakers.

621. Insurance Conference Planners Association. Another group of those who hire speakers and trainers.

622. Instructional Systems Associations

623. National Retail Federation

624.   National Association of Women Business Owners, and other groups of business owners.

Strategic Alliances and Partnerships: Share Leads and Support

625.   Partner with others in a strategic alliance to share leads. Never do lead sharing on dates that have been booked by speakers' bureaus.

626.   Form a consortium. Team with other noncompeting people to form a consortium of those types of experts your market share will find useful. A consortium implies a bit of a more formal relationship than an alliance. However, the difference can be all in the name. Use whichever best tickles the fancy of your customer base.

627.   Some alliances pay each other a referral fee for referral of good business opportunities.

628.   Collaborate with other industry leaders to coauthor books, and other products.

629.   Develop friendships, with no thought of profit, with other professionals who are doing what you want to do. From honest and sincere friendships will come the greatest rewards, many of which turn out to be monetary.

Sales and Negotiating Skills

630.   You must become adept at sales skills if you intend to become a paid professional speaker, trainer, or presenter. You may be the best presenter and the greatest expert in the world. But you will generate no income if the word *sell* bothers you. Don't think *sell*, think *serve*. To serve, you just think in terms of your prospects' needs and wants. To learn what their needs and wants are, all you have to do is to ask them gentle questions. Listen and take careful notes on what your prospects want.

631.   Give your prospects what they ask for—joyfully and gladly. You must want them to have the very best.

Business Card Magic

632. Your product is your business card. Everything it is, is the essence of your career.

633. Always carry your business cards with you and exchange with potential customers.

634. It is much more important to get clients' contact information than to give them yours.

635. Each time you visit a client, get the business card of one other person.

636. Create business card–size versions of your program flyers and products. People rarely keep flyers, but they often keep business cards.

637. List your seminars and books on the back of your business card.

638. Put a coupon on the back of your business card that gives clients a discount to one of your products or programs.

639. Print up business cards in very small quantities with your name, and the name of the bureau that sent you to the event. Give them out at dates for which you are booked.

Fees and Negotiating

640. Have a small form made up and ready when potential customers call. List who, what, where, when, why, and how. When they ask you to speak for their group, smile and say, "Tell me more." After you get all the rest of the information, ask this question: "What is your budget for this program?"

641. When clients say they need to negotiate and reduce your fee, do not give them a bargain price for no viable reason. Find a way to exchange value for value. When you do this, customers will have respect for you and the quality of the services you offer. If you do not value your work, no one else will either.

Reasons to Consider a Lower Fee

642. Showcase opportunities to prospective buyers: See if working for this client involves marketing opportunities for other speaking, consulting, or product sales. Audiences of speakers' bureau representatives, meeting planners, and association or corporate executives fall into this group.

643. If the client has a service or product that is of real value to you, barter part or all of your fee in exchange. Speakers have traded speeches and seminars for new automobiles, long-distance dialing credits, boats, and many other valuable things.

644. Exchange part of your fee for an ad in the client's company or association publication if the audience might prove a good market for your books, cassettes, products, and other services. An ad is a concrete value that has a price you can negotiate.

645. Exchange part of your fee for an ad in the client's event program brochure. These ads can bring you cash sales. An ad is a concrete value that has a price you can negotiate.

646. Trade should be taken at least in full dollar-to-dollar retail value of the item, or even more. The markup on items the client barters is often 75 percent over the wholesale cost. Exchange your normal listed full fee for the value in retail list price on their items.

647. Sell a large number of products with the presentation. If the buyer prepurchases a large number of your products as training materials or gifts for attendees, offer a volume discount. For example, if your regular fee is $3000, and the client needs 1000 of your cassette albums on the subject to present to the attendees, and the albums retail for $89.95 each, you might offer them for 50 percent off retail with your full speaking fee. Or, discount your speaking fee to $2000, and offer 30 percent off the retail album price.

648. The client usually has a separate budget for educational materials outside of the meeting. See if you can negotiate product sales as part of that budget.

649.   If you are skilled at several topics, do several at the same meeting or event. Offer to do one of your other topics at a lower or no fee if clients buy the first one at full price. They get the advantage of paying only one set of expenses (plane tickets and hotel rooms) and gain an additional program at a bargain price.

650.   Sometimes there is another budget for special subgroups attending an event (spouses, children, managers, presidents, etc.). Find out who is in charge of this program, suggest they call the person in charge of spouse and youth programs or let them know you will call them, and see if you can work out the trade. The client is able to combine the two budgets.

651.   Sell multiple dates in the same contract. If the client needs several speakers or seminar leaders during the year for different audiences and/or locations, offer to present a series of performances at a lesser fee.

652.   When clients tell you, "Cut your fee on this talk, and then we might use you in a series," you reply, "This program will cost full price, but I will be glad to add a clause stating: 'If a series contract is signed within one year of this date, $____ will be deducted from the series price.'" Remember, the person you are negotiating with may not be with the company or association next year, or even next month. So get full price for this program and put the future discount into the contract. While it may seem tempting to accept a cut rate on the date at hand with the hope of a future contract, it is not a good idea. This offer might be made only to reduce your fee, with no real intention of offering a future series. In addition, you might pass up other bookings because you are holding a series of dates.

653.   Another way to negotiate multiple contracts is to write all of the dates of the series on the original contract, with a deposit due on all of them, including the first one. The balance on each contract date would be paid two weeks before each program day. Stay in touch, and bill the client appropriately, with a copy of the contract sent each time. Bookkeepers also change.

654. If customers are sincere in their promises, they will not hesitate to sign a firm contract for a series at the lower rate. If the dates are not set, just write into the contract, "four programs within ____ [their time frame]."

655. Sell a set of articles. Offer to write a set of perhaps 12 monthly articles for your client's own publication. Discount your regular price for the articles because you offer volume of 12 or 24 articles, but charge full price for the presentation or training.

656. A pay-in-advance discount is offered by most suppliers in most industries. Most businesses, big or small, like a discount. Consider offering a discount for paying 100 percent immediately, including expenses, with the signing of the contract. Then, after the event, you are not chasing money, but are able to be in position to do follow-up. Besides, when you are calling to chase money, you cannot be asking for referrals, another booking, or a thank-you letter.

657. See if the company will pay for transportation, hotel rooms, and meals for both you and your spouse that extend beyond the dates of the meeting so that you can have a vacation. Often, a large convention has complementary rooms and discounts on airfares. This is a perk that costs them very little, but can mean a wonderful time together for you at a beautiful resort, and has a solid, tangible, negotiable value.

658. No matter whether you charge for each item included or offer a package deal, use an itemized bill that spells out the high value of each item the customer will receive. Have the invoice say, "Actual value," and then the special negotiated fee you will be charging the customer.

659. Sometimes you might make a great deal more by taking a lesser fee but having a percentage of the profits from the event.

Keep Your Promises and Remember Details

660. Write down anything you tell customers you will do. It is very difficult to repair the bad impression you leave in their minds when you forget details.

Cold-calling Clients

661. Cold calling is the least effective of all types of sales in this industry, unless you have qualified your leads before calling.

662. Be quick when cold calling. Know exactly what you intend to say before you call. Listening to a long, drawn-out prescripted pitch just annoys people. Instead, be quick, and to the point.

Buyers Are Impressed When You Try to Sell Them Because in a Sales Call . . .

663. You know the audience and the industry of the person you are talking to. You do not just say you do, your words show you do.

664. You take an interest in the group for which you are being considered.

665. You relate experiences with similar groups.

666. You have referrals appropriate to the group or industry.

You Turn off Clients During Sales Calls When . . .

667. You only talk about yourself and how you can help the group, without asking about the group. Ninety nine percent of every call you must spend listening and learning. You must remember to ask about and find out their special needs.

668. You let the call go on over four minutes. Listen, don't talk! If they are leading you forward, then stay with them.

669. You keep calling after you have been told they will get in touch if they are interested.

It's a Numbers Game: Don't Give up, Follow Up

670.   You will not be able to turn every call you make into a booking. Many say final odds are 50 prospect phone calls to 1 booking. If you want to present three paid programs a week, you will need to call 150 prospects a week. This may not seem like a genius idea, but genius goes around disguised as intelligent persistence. Remember—Don't give up, follow up.

671.   Remember that a "no" now can turn into a "yes" later, particularly if you succeed in making a lasting impression. If you get angry or feel defeated, you may overlook many opportunities to change a turndown into a booking or create opportunities for future appearances. The buyer may have wanted you, but was vetoed by someone else in the company.

672.   If you are rejected this time, mention that if anything should happen to the speaker they have chosen, you would be delighted to stand in.

673.   Call your contact when the meeting is over and ask how it went, or drop a card saying you hope all went well.

674.   Ask the buyer who rejected you for a reference for a group he or she knows would be suitable for your material. Buyers know each other.

675.   Ask for honest feedback about why they choose another speaker. "Do you think it was my style? My content? Or perhaps my promotional materials?" Do not argue with their assessment, just listen and take notes.

BECOMING FAMOUS: ARTICLES, NEWSLETTERS, MAGAZINES, AND THE PRESS

Where to Find Media Contacts

676.   Get media referrals. People who work in any sort of media often know other people in the same field who may be interested in your topic. Don't be afraid to ask them for a referral to a noncompetitor show or publication.

677. Call the local newspaper and radio and TV stations. Pick up your phone book, and look online.

678. Watch the mail, the media, and everything that comes to hand. And ask yourself these questions:

- Is there a possibility here for a story or interview?
- How can I be of service to these people?

679. Use a PR firm.

680. Check with the public library reference librarian for other directories of media contacts.

681. A great source for media is the *Gale Directory of Print and Broadcast Media,* located at the library.

682. You can also access Gale information online. The Gale Database of Publications and Broadcast Media is a comprehensive file containing detailed information on 67,500 newspapers, magazines, journals, periodicals, directories, newsletters, and radio, television, and cable stations and systems. You purchase this for a fee.

683. Use a newswire service. Go to Google.com and use the search term *newswire.*

684. Wherever you are searching for media, such as online or at the library, check multiple categories.

685. News

686. Directory of newsletters

687. Trade journals

688. Major publications

689. Newspapers

690. E-zines and e-news

691. Television stations

692. Radio stations

693. Broadcast companies

694.   Anything to do with your topic, and the preceding ideas

695.   Anything to do with your target industry, and the preceding ideas

Get the Media to Use Your Material

696.   Obtaining free publicity in the media is an effective way to build your fame as an expert and attract paid bookings. However, keep in mind this all-important fact about newspapers, magazines, and radio and television stations: they do not want to promote you. They are in the business of *selling* advertisements to people who want promotion. However, they do want to deliver fascinating, exciting, helpful material to their readers or audiences, so that their circulation or ratings will increase and enable them to profit by charging higher advertising rates. If you view the media business from their side, you will quickly see that if you help them get such information to their readers, listeners, or viewers, the publicity for you and your topic will naturally follow. You will be identified as a top resource in your field, a celebrity expert.

697.   Only call the media when you have something newsworthy to report. Don't be guilty of the "boy who cried wolf" syndrome. The media will soon tune you out unless you have serious and interesting tidbits for them.

698.   Target the media's audience, style, and timetable. You can often use almost the same article for different fields by rearranging and changing the material to fit each publication. Newsletters for dentists, for example, are not in competition with those for doctors, yet they have similar needs and would welcome a very similar article.

699.   Attract the media's attention by getting the "you" attitude into your public relations, promotions, and advertising. "How **You** Can Overcome . . ." says "you" outright. But titles like "New Method to Obtain . . ." clearly imply "you."

700. Never call a press person and ask, "Did you get my press release?" They get hundreds. These are words that just annoy them, unless they called you and asked you for the release.

701. Grab those first few seconds on the phone (or in front of their eyes on your press releases) and ask, "Would your viewers like to learn how to . . . ?" "Would your listeners like to know the answer to . . . ?"

702. Can you get the essence of what you want to tell the media representative into one short sentence? No? Then you are not ready to call. Write it all out, then pare it down, then pare it down some more. Have that one sentence it front of you when you call.

703. Test every line and every word of all copy you write to make sure there is a benefit for the audience in every sentence.

704. Listen to and/or read the media in which you want exposure. Know them before you approach them.

705. Call the producer or editor of the programs or article sections pertaining to your topic. Ask if they are interested and if they like the way your slant on your topic matches up with their audience.

706. Connect to what is current: watch the stories that appear in the media. Ask yourself, "How can I tie my expertise in with that and help these people?"

707. Keep in touch. Send press releases, notes, and updates via mail, e-mail, and fax, two or three times a year. Not enough to be a pest, but enough to let them know you are out there.

How to Get the Press to Notice You

708. The press is often more interested in a story about your topic instead of one about you.

709. Controversy sells. The *Star* and *National Enquirer* are read by millions of people each week. People love something out of the ordinary and nontraditional:

the same old thing is boring. People love to talk about the unusual, eccentric, or bizarre. It's entertainment, not information alone that sells. (Tip from George Roman, Beverly Hills Love Guru)

710.   Take a survey. Be the expert on those results. Often the material you develop in your survey can become a book, a report, an audio or video album, or a CD. There is nothing like talking to the people who are out in the business world to find out what is really going on.

711.   Search the census. There are all kinds of interesting facts in the U.S. and state censuses. No matter what your topic, you can find facts to back it up and make an interesting news release. The U.S. census is found online at www.census.gov, with the topics listed from A to Z. One trainer I know used a statistic that said the entire budget for one bomb would feed one of our smaller states for a year! He had the actual bomb and state information. This fact fit in very nicely with his topic. Reporters love statistics because they help give a story perspective.

712.   Get a calendar of all of the zillions of special days, weeks, and months. Groundhog Day and Black History Month get a great deal of press, but there are many, many others. These are easy ways to get a press release out.

713.   What events are happening in your area? Use a local publicity angle. Is something in your area causing talk in the community? Put up a Web site quickly that can take a poll on this subject. The press will be interested and let the public know. Have a small link at the bottom that leads to more about your products.

714.   What's in the news at a national level? What is making the headlines? If you can tie in what you do with that topic, you will be amazed at the press's interest.

715.   Any item on the legitimate newswires such as Associated Press or UPI can generate a massive response. Most electronic releases go directly to editorial computers, are preferred by editors over print media, and receive more immediate attention than direct mail or faxes. What's more, an electronic release lives on in the database for years. However, you must have a great hook in your publicity release or it will be a waste of time.

716. When you have a good story in your local media, ask them to submit the story to the wire services.

Awards and Lists

717. Give awards. Select people to receive the "___ Award For Excellence in ___." (You fill in the blanks to compliment your area of expertise.) These awards are given to executives and celebrities and are a way to get your company name into the press. It always brings you to the attention of top executives.

718. Create a hall of fame. It does not necessarily need to be an actual building, it can be a Web site. Being inducted into a hall of fame is very newsworthy. Of course this must be related to your area of expertise.

719. Create a "best" or "worst" list. If possible, give your list an intriguing name instead of just best or worst. Rank the 5, 10, or even 20 best or worst of a topic that ties into your area of expertise, product, or service.

720. Create a list of interesting facts about ___. In addition to the census, check research available in libraries or online and of course your own extensive personal knowledge base of your subject. Create a list of the 5, 10, or more appropriate, interesting facts.

721. Find an intriguing name for your list that sells by simply using your thesaurus! These are a part of most word processors. I just typed in *simply*, hit the thesaurus button, and was given a list that included more interesting synonyms such as un-arduous!

Standing out in the Crowd

722. Be the only one of your kind; being unusual, rare, or notable is often an easy path to enticing the press to you. Your unique quality must be something that not only sets you apart from the competition, but is powerful, memorable, and at the same time communicates a benefit for your customer.

723.   Look unusual. Think of ways to look unusual and to help people to remember your name and your topic. Use a special color in your business stationery, business cards, or presentation kit. Movie actress Kim Novak became famous for always wearing shades of lavender. Some speakers always wear a hat.

724.   Work with an unusual prop. Dottie Walters uses a dragon puppet in her presentations. Harvey Mackay, the outstanding speaker and author of *Swim With the Sharks Without Being Eaten Alive,* gives meeting planners, bureau owners, and attendees little gold shark pins.

725.   Do the unusual. Others that are easily remembered are those that have been the first to perform a feat such as walking across America backward or in a wheelchair.

Publicity Releases that Get Results

726.   Sum up the most important thrust of the release in the headline in capital letters. Assume readers will only read that one line.

727.   You must get the reporter to call you for more information. Write long headlines that say it all. This is often all reporters will read. If the headline says everything needed to entice and inspire, they may read the rest.

728.   Although you should and must be filled with passion about your topic to make it in this industry, to qualify as news, your information must be objective. Your zealous, passionate push of your issues will get an exasperated sigh and a toss in the trash. Even if you are 100 percent in the right of your opinion, that much passion in news releases reads like advertising and traditional media professionals won't use them.

729. Do passion-filled news releases for the "rags." Although the traditional media will most likely give your zeal a trash toss, the "rags" might love it! Before you scoff, these rags can claim to be the most read publications in the world, and can be the greatest exposure you will ever receive.

730. Put the source of the release in the upper left corner of your paper. This is the name, address, phone number, and e-mail of the person to contact for further information. The contact person may be you or someone at your PR service. Put the release date, typed in capital letters, slightly below the source information and on the opposite (right) side of the page.

731. If you are sending the release via mail or fax, use standard 8½ × 11-inch sheets of paper. Smaller or larger sizes are hard for media people to store. Use only one side of the paper. Use a fine grade of paper. A color other than white may help you stand out in the crowd, but stay in the warm spectrum.

Keep the length of the release to one page whenever possible. If you must use more, type (*MORE*) at the bottom. Staple all pages at the top left. On the last page, type ### or -30- or *END*. Your releases should be typed double-spaced. Leave a three-inch margin on the top of the first page and leave margins on each side that are wide enough for editing.

732. Use the advice of Rudyard Kipling.

> *I keep six honest serving men,*
> *They taught me all I knew.*
> *Their names were What and Where and When,*
> *And How and Why and Who.*

Make sure to get all of your "serving men" in the first paragraph of your news releases. Put the most important and exciting one at the head of the story.

733. Find out how far in advance each contact wants your information. Lead time for a daily paper may be three or four weeks. For a monthly magazine, figure on three or four months. Ask. Send it out when they want it.

734.   Don't pass off nonoriginal material as exclusive.

735.   Don't try to make an advertisement for yourself out of an article or release. Make it fascinating news for readers instead. Make the trail that leads back to you subtle.

736.   When you get the release all written, imagine an exasperated news editor looking at you, the release in his hands, saying, "So what? Why are our readers going to be excited to hear any of this?"

737.   Keep your news release mailing list up to date. Post changes as you receive them. Media people like to see releases addressed to them rather than to their predecessors.

Get Your Articles out into the World

738.   Watch for bylines on articles that have almost any connection to your area of expertise. Call the publications and ask for the writer of those specific stories. The author may be on staff or may work on speculation. In either case, when you reach the writer, say how much you enjoyed the article.

739.   As you are booked to speak, ask clients which trade journals they read. Make it a point to locate and contact those publications with an article offer to develop more bookings in your field. It is often much easier to get started writing for trade journals than for major publications.

740.   Every article sent out by you must be filled with interesting facts. Interesting ideas, or ways people can improve their way of doing business or their lives, often get published. Blatant commercialism will not get published.

741.   Find ways to get others to write articles about you in traditional newspapers.

742.   Find ways to get others to write articles about you in magazines. Check online and at the library. Find all the little magazines that are hungry for stories.

743.   Find ways to get others to write articles about you in their newsletters. These are much easier to get into than newspapers and magazines.

744.   Find ways to get others to write articles about you; submit these to e-zines.

745.   Have others quote you as an expert. This is normally much more interesting and more newsworthy than just articles about you. Your opinions or quotes must be within quote marks and attributed to you as the expert; otherwise the news media get turned off. Even better would be impartial third parties quoting what they have heard about you or your philosophy.

746.   Write articles yourself that show you off as a sought-after expert in your area of expertise. Work on having these printed in traditional newspapers.

747.   Write articles yourself that show you off as a sought-after expert in your area of expertise. Work on having these printed in magazines.

748.   Write articles yourself that show you off as a sought-after expert in your area of expertise. Work on having these printed in newsletters.

749.   Put your copyright on all articles you send out, along with a way to contact you. Sometimes you will get paid for them, sometimes you won't. Either way, they are very valuable.

750.   Create articles that you hope will be passed around for free! Say at the beginning: "You may use this in your e-news, newsletters, or Web site, if you include [your contact hyperlink]."

751.   Go to Google.com. Type in your area of expertise and *e-zine*. A huge list will appear. Contact these people and offer an article written by someone else about you. See the ideas this section on using Google.com to find them.

752.   In Google, type in your area of expertise and *e-news*.

753.   In Google, type in your area of expertise and *newsletter*.

754.   In Google, type in your area of expertise and *magazine*.

What Do You Do When They Want to Quote You for Free?

755.   If someone asks you for a quote in their publication, product, or seminar, say yes! At least your ideas are being credited to you. This person is willing to help spread the word about your expertise. If you say no, the harsh reality is that people are going to use "adaptations" of the things you have said and written—whether they ask your permission or not.

756.   When people ask to quote you, realize that the audience they are trying to reach is a group you are trying to reach as well. Offer to do an additional step, and give them a bunch more neat free stuff—perhaps a whole page they can reprint and insert in their workbooks, or a copy of your newsletter. You can include the URL of where they can get a free download of a chapter of your book or find free articles or ways to sign up for free tips. Make a neat list of these great valuable freebies that others will want to give out to their attendees.

Tips for Radio Interviews

757.   The benefits of a radio interview to your speaking career include promoting your topic, your availability to be booked on that topic, and perhaps telephone numbers, books, album prices, and ordering information. Arrange with the producer in advance for the opportunity to mention these things. Some show producers prefer to have the host plug your free gift and products, not you.

758.   Before the interview begins, you should write several important things on a big piece of paper and have it in front of you:

- Key words and phrases from your topic. This will serve as a reminder of the things you want to get on the air.

- The name of the host. Call the host(s) by name during the interview.

- The studio's emergency telephone number.
- The giveaway listeners can have if they call you.
- How listeners can reach you.

759. Sometimes a host will go off on a tangent subject that has nothing to do with you or your topic. Be funny and warm, but pull the conversation back to your topic. You might answer, "That reminds me of a question I was asked when I spoke in New York recently." Then you talk about the topic again.

760. Make it a point to have yourself introduced as not only the expert in your field, but a professional speaker on the subject. Drop a line in your printed material and articles, or a remark during the verbal interviews: "My audiences often ask me that . . ." "Someone in my audience in Japan asked me that same question." Then answer the question. This positions you as a speaker.

When They Say No

761. Be nice! So many media people complain that people are hostile to them when they can't use their materials. If they need to close a door on you, don't padlock it on your side by pouting. Just say, "Love to help next time!"

762. If they say no or they aren't sure, ask, "Would you give me a tip? Is there any part of my topic that is intriguing to your demographic? How might I change the focus to make it more interesting to your listeners/readers, etc.?"

ROAD WARRIORS: BRAINY BUSINESS AND BALANCE

763. The reality of a speaker's life is that you are the "commodity" that is for sale, and that commodity is often on the road. You do not necessarily need an office with a staff. You do need a way to be in quick contact with clients and potential clients while you are traveling. You must become a traveling virtual office. This means a computer, modem, and electronic versions of your materials and forms that travel with you. Many speakers are able to easily handle the rest from a spare room or corner of their own homes with the assistance of their spouse or a part-time staff person.

764. If you do become overwhelmed with work, a good rule is to hire people to do tasks at which you are no good (or just plain don't like).

Schedules: Are You Available?

765. Speakers, trainers, and seminar leaders sell dates. Those dates on your calendar are your inventory—your stock in trade—as are your products. You must have a quick, efficient method to track dates, times, and locations of your speaking engagements, meetings with potential clients, and other important matters.

766. Keep a map of your country and world map with time zones, zip codes, and telephone area codes close to you and to whomever else is checking your schedule.

Travel Scheduling Challenges

767. You cannot book a date unless you check carefully that you can meet the travel scheduling challenges. Look at the dates on either side of the proposed event. Note your location the day before, and the travel time from venue to venue, to be sure you have time to move from one day's engagement to the next, allowing for canceled flights and delays. This can be done in seconds using one of the many online travel sites.

768. Figure the estimated travel time involved so that you will arrive refreshed and alert. Allow for late plane arrivals to be sure you will have time to get some rest. It is always best to arrive the night before an event.

769. Never accept a date if there is only one flight available to get to the engagement! If that flight is canceled, you let down a great many people. Ask them to schedule you later in their program or on another day. If they can't, just say no. You will make a much better impression declining this date.

770. When booking flights, never take the last possible plane that will get you to the speech exactly on time. If that flight is canceled, you have no other options left to get you there. You are being paid not just for the time you are present on the platform, but for taking the personal responsibility to be at the presentation site refreshed and on time (more than on time, be there before the event planners get there!), ready to give the best performance of your life.

771. Consider the time of year the meeting is being held. Are there likely to be any weather problems? What are alternate means of transportation in case of blizzard or storm?

772. Check the real time it takes to arrive at the venue in question. For example, on a map of the United States, Wyoming looks close to Denver. Denver is easy to get to from most other major cities. Therefore, you may figure that you should be able to make a Wyoming date on time with no problem. But this may not be so. Check with your travel agent. How many local flights actually go to that area of Wyoming from Denver? How far is the venue from the airport? What is the ground transportation situation? Until you know the answers to these questions, you cannot accept a booking.

773. Carry with you the clothes and materials you must have to give the speech. As "Cowboy" Bob Walters always said, "There are only two kinds of luggage: carry-on and lost." Find bags that you can carry on comfortably. Keep a set of the smallest-size necessities (toothpaste, brush, etc.) packed and ready to go, and pare these necessities down to a minimum. Also pack a small travel steam iron. The dry cleaning facilities may be closed when you arrive. You can usually ask the hotel staff to supply an ironing board in your hotel room.

774.   If you must ship your materials ahead, have an alternate plan when they are lost (which they often will be). Using second-day air, for arrival two days before you get to the venue, is the best way to ensure that it actually will be there when you are. Call the day before and confirm the package's arrival with the bell captain at the hotel or conference center to which it was sent.

Smart Calendar Tips

775.   Calendar information must be easily accessible, with the data available to you in less than 10 seconds. This most likely means a computer system.

776.   Regardless of the calendar system you use, it must be quick and accessible to all members of your teams.

777.   One person and/or calendar must be the master that is checked before a date can be confirmed for you if you are on the road and book dates; otherwise you may be double-booked.

778.   Use a three-or-more-year calendar. You will often be booked a year or more in advance. Even as a beginning professional, you must be able to track your future whereabouts several years ahead of time.

779.   There are online calendars you can add to your Web site that can be accessible to you, your home team, and your customers. You can make changes from the road, as can your team back home.

What to Do if You're Already Booked

780.   If you are unavailable for a date, suggest the client use you for the following year's program. If the client agrees, send the contract out immediately with your usual deposit clause. You will find that next year's calendar fills quickly with contracts if you use this method.

781.   For all dates for which you are unavailable, offer to help the client find another speaker. See "Sharing and Networking to Gain Referrals" in Chap. 3.

782. Tell clients you will have your favorite speakers' bureau find a suitable speaker for this year. This will please your bureau and encourage bureaus to remember you for other paid dates.

Miscellaneous Ideas to Create Income While on the Road

783. Create marketing letters to your own list of customers, or to a purchase list. These letters include information and testimonials aimed at a specific group. Give these, along with a mailing schedule for the next six months, to a secretarial service and put them on autopilot. This way something goes out on a regular basis. This marketing works without you, while you are out working.

784. Talk to your phone company about a phone service or system that gives your callers options when they call in. The caller can press one button and hear the automated catalog you have there for them. These systems allow callers to place orders 24 hours a day— some even generate an invoice automatically! Fax on demand can also be a part of this system, so your caller can request your bios, speech outlines, and so on. Of course, your Web site should be set up to take orders 24/7.

785. Once an order is taken, someone needs to be back home filling your product orders. You will find it least expensive to have this done through an inexpensive part-time person rather than a fulfillment house.

How Accessible to Be from the Road

786. How easy is it to find you? Make it easy for customers to buy you. We live in an information age that has all kinds of ways to keep you accessible to your clients. The world no longer waits for you to return to your home office to answer requests. An answer to a proposed date needs to be done now.

Equipment for the Road Warrior

787. You must have a laptop computer with a fax modem, e-mail setup, and a cell phone.

788. You must know how to use a laptop computer with a fax modem, e-mail, and a cell phone! Do what it takes to learn how to operate these tools.

789. If you do not have someone answering your phones at home, then you must have an answering device you can access from the road, and/or forward your calls to your cell phone from your home office phone.

790. Create equipment that you can use on and off the road seamlessly. You will be writing your books, doing your research, and creating new materials while in airports and in your home office. Buy your equipment with this in mind.

Team up with Other Speakers for an Office

791. If it is not convenient for you to set up a home office, consider teaming up with other speakers to rent office space. New office complexes frequently offer their tenants answering services, copy and facsimile machines, and the use of conference rooms.

Software

792. You will write workbooks and articles. They are mandatory in the speaking/training/consulting profession. I suggest Microsoft Word. Why? Because I use it! There are many others, maybe just as good or better, but I have been delighted with MS Word. Whichever software you choose, features you need if you intend to do large documents, like books and workbooks, are:

- Automatic indexing

- Automatic outlining

- Automatic table of contents

Automatic outlining is a mandatory feature for anyone doing serious writing.

Most of your charts and tables for your presentations and workbooks can be created in a good word processing program like Microsoft Word.

793. Many of your written items (workbooks, articles, books) can be converted to PDF files. PDFs are what most e-books are. It is simple to use, most often as an add-on to all of your other programs. Your profit on e-books can be enormous.

794. You can store your entire stock of promotional materials, presentation kits, and research files on your computer, and have them on the road with you. If you have the originals with you, then creating customized marketing materials is instantaneous. Then you can e-mail the files to your customers immediately from any place you are that has a telephone line (unless you are wireless; then all you need is a signal).

Set up a Business Communication System: Voice mail, E-mail, Faxes, Phones

795. If you are in business, you need to be on your phone. If you have only one line, this means your fax is then unusable. If the fax is in use on the one phone line, you are unusable. If your computer is getting your e-mail, you and your fax are unusable. Set up a system that allows phone, fax, and e-mail and you to be constantly available. The answer to this challenge changes monthly. Talk to your phone company.

796. Consider a service you can use as a fax that is actually an online source. This way you can collect your faxes, no matter where you are. These cost from $4 to $20 a month, much less than an additional phone line, and accessible from the road.

Communication Efficiency Tips

797. It is much preferred that you give personal service to your customers, not automated service. But even an automated service is much better than a busy signal or a phone that rings with no one to answer.

798. If you are on one line, you need a system that allows the calls to rotate to the next line—which you have set up with voice mail if no one is available to answer it. The phone companies in most cities now supply a message center that will do this automatically for you.

799.   Do not use call waiting on your business line! If you have just begun your speaking career and are still running your operation with little or no staff, have your calls roll right into your voice mail.

800.   Teach your team to answer your phone with the right words and a warm, smiling, positive tone. You and your company are judged by how well your phone is answered. A grumpy teenager with a mouth full of peanut butter who mumbles, "No, dunno where she is. Call back." (Slam!) does not project a good business image and likely will lose the prospect.

801.   Install a separate phone, perhaps a cell phone, for your business to avoid family problems.

802.   When you decide on an answering system, select one that continues recording as long as the caller is speaking and does not cut him or off in midsentence at a preset time. Ask for a voice-activated system.

803.   Keep your recorded greeting brief and businesslike. Avoid music introductions, phony voices, or poems in your message. These can be very irritating to clients or speakers' bureaus who want to reach you. Get to the point!

804.   Avoid phone tag. The message on your telephone answering system must ask for a complete message; also, it should update your callers on your location, schedule, and when they can expect a call back.

Alternatives to the Traditional Office Staff

805.   Today it is much easier to work without staff than it was a few years ago. Still, most people in this industry have someone they can count on to be at the phones from 9 to 5. Many use a family member or someone in the community who wants to work at home. This person must be supplied with a cell phone. You can forward calls to that phone when you need to turn yours off.

Then they only need a pad of paper, and your calendar, and they can run your business while at the grocery store! When they get home, they can mail requests for information, fulfill product orders, and enter names into your database.

806. Before you bring in a staff person, create a list of qualifications and skills that you require and a list of other skills that would be beneficial but not necessarily required. All of these should center around those things that you dislike doing, do not have time to do, or are not very good at. All of them should revolve around how they sound on the phone and if they can get your materials in the mail.

807. There are several companies out there that act as your office staff and are willing to work for a very small fee plus a commission. Some call themselves remote office management companies, or speakers' offices.

808. Ask a secretary in your circle to consider working for you in the evenings and weekends at his or her home. This person should know your wants, habits, and dislikes and be well suited to assist you by doing such tasks as going to the post office to pick up and drop off mail, processing mail and orders for you, and making routine phone calls.

809. Try using professional outside vendors and service companies for secretarial, copying, mailing, answering service, fax delivery, collating, and bookkeeping needs. Some secretarial services will send out your press kit and other promotional materials. They keep your letterhead stationery on hand so that you can dictate letters to them over the phone, by fax, or by audio cassette.

810. Hire temp workers. That way you can "hire" them and "fire" them as business requires.

811. Find an up-and-coming speaker, trainer, or consultant who wants to learn about office management and marketing of a professional. Allow him or her to apprentice with you and learn about your office.

812.   College interns can be a great, inexpensive asset. Get interns who can't graduate unless they finish up the project they're doing with you and make sure that project pushes your career ahead—not just theirs.

813.   Hire people who want to work out of their homes. It will cost you less.

814.   If you use family as staff, include them in your goals, plans, and rewards. That way they will be fervent in their support rather than resentful toward your business. Commission incentives for your family team are a big motivator! Don't bring your family in and expect them to work for free. If you are willing to pay an outsider, then show the same respect to every member of your family when you expect them to do the same task. "Well, you are my son! Don't you care about me?" is a poor reward for a task well done.

815.   Tell others how good your staff is at any given task when they can overhear you.

816.   One of the first people you may want to add to your growing staff is an inside marketing person who is good at selling your services and products.

817.   Don't worry about what your marketing person looks like! How often will your buyers see him or her? Hire your marketer on the basis of phone personality. Put your phone number in the ad. Have candidates call you. Listen to their voice projection and their telephone personality. Consider having them call a private line with an answering device. Your message should give simple instructions about leaving their resume on the voice message machine. You want to know how their personality sounds, and if they can follow instructions.

Why Your Staff Is Driving Your Business Away

818.   New staff members often drive customers away unintentionally. They don't have the knowledge or authority to make decisions or even know your schedule or how it works.

819. There are many speakers, trainers, and consultants who are not booked because their staff members are not polite or act like customers are a difficulty. One of the wisest investments you will make in this industry is hiring happy, customer-focused people.

Balancing Your Career and Family

Once you become successful, you will be on the road a great deal. A growing, successful family takes just as much nurturing as your career does. You will need to be creative and persistent to include your family in your life. Your greatest profits in your life will be from healthy relationships you have with your family. Decide what your priorities and values are. What good is it to have a successful speaking career if you lose your family and/or health in the process?

- Call home daily and talk to all members of the family.

- Send little notes and/or cards in the mail to each family member. Nothing is more personal than a written note.

- Plan time with your family that has nothing to do with you, but is strictly for them.

820. Treat friends and family with the same seriousness as clients when you schedule work. Schedule your family time. Not just a vague time, but a date in your day planner. Get their permission to reschedule.

821. Set clear limits on numbers of workdays you will take, and stick to that number. Once you have enough work, consider saying "no" to certain days that will be family time—perhaps weekends.

822. Speak less but at higher fees, if possible.

823. Take your spouse and/or children along with you on some of your speaking engagements.

824.   Do not commit yourself to business activities when you're off the road. Take all possible work—such as reading, research, and follow-up calls—to complete on the plane or in the hotel. Don't have it waiting for you when you return.

Staying Married

825.   Remember the reasons why you married in the first place.

826.   Make the needs of your relationship more important than the business.

827.   Make the decision your spouse is *the one* and divorce is not an option.

Procrastination and Organization

828.   Start organizing yourself and your business with an organizer. If you don't have one, get one, now! It must live with you as a part of your life. You need to set a completion date for all your plans and write them in your organizer.

829.   Plan several years in advance. Use your planning system every day, all day long.

830.   Determine the long-term payoff for each day you spend. According to Victor Kiam, "Procrastination is opportunity's natural assassin." Procrastinators wait for the mood to strike them before tackling a task. Get started regardless of your feelings and your fears. Dive right into productive action, whether the mood is there or not.

831.   It's OK to "Just Say No." Rather than feeling that you are a bad person or unworthy, just say no.

832.   Keep your commitments to yourself.

833.   Focus on your goals. Many speakers have told me they missed a great deal of opportunity along the way because they did not carefully focus at the beginning.

Time Savers

834. Unclutter your work surfaces on a regular basis—probably daily.

835. Don't handle something more than once. As you look at it, deal with it by forcing yourself to take one of three options: do, dump, or delegate!

836. Those things you can't do, dump, or delegate, put on one of your lists, then add them to a to-do list.

837. Reduce go-between phone calls with conference calls. This will also reduce the total time spent in communication and in misunderstandings. When using conference calls, make sure to let the people involved know in advance so they will be prepared. They are much more excited and feel the call to be more important when it is a conference call.

838. Do more of those things that are the best use of your time to move you toward your goals. Do less of those things that are of little value.

Use Wait Times and Road Time Effectively

839. I use a database to keep and sort my projects. As ideas occur, I switch to that and add the ideas in.

840. At the airport you can plug your computer into a terminal and download your e-mails, send and collect orders, and find research information.

841. Airplane time can be the best available for writing your books and other products.

842. You are on the road because you are working, which means you will be fatigued. Create goals with realistic expectations on the road. Then accomplishing those will leave you with a feeling of fulfillment.

843. Plan and create new products on your computer on the road.

844. View new venues for seminar sites.

845. Always meet with the sales staff of the hotel venue; make sure they know who you are and what you do.

They have close contact with buyers of meetings and can often make suggestions. Leave your card and get theirs.

846.   Before you hit the road, call the venue at which you are presenting. Talk to the sales manager. Offer to do a 30-minute program for the sales staff. This puts you in their minds as great authority on a given subject, and they are more apt to refer you to their clients.

Double Your Income with Products and Tools of the Trade

DOUBLE YOUR INCOME WITH PRODUCTS

Products are valuable additional income extensions to your body of knowledge. They not only become at least half of your income, but are also scouts that constantly direct prospects back to you.

847. Spend what it takes—time and money—to get a book on the best-seller list very early in your career!

Tips to Create Products that Generate Income

848. Make a list of what things would be beneficial in assisting businesses and individuals to get the job done more efficiently as you discuss it in your materials and speeches. This is the basis for creating your products.

849. If such products already exist, consider acting as a distributor for those products and selling them yourself.

850. If you can think of a way to do these things even better, or in a newer way than existing products, then create a version yourself!

851. Whenever people say to you, "I need to know more about _____," you have the seeds of a product.

852. Constantly gather new material and update the material you already have on your topic. Soon you will have enough for some type of product.

853. Think in terms of performance support and expertise on demand as you create products. Businesses are very reluctant to let people off work to attend a seminar. Training materials that continue the educational process while the employee is on the job are the easiest of all products to sell.

Gathering Material

854. When you see articles, hear someone speak, watch the news, or read a quotation, ideas will come to mind that tie into your material. Write them down or tear the articles out and store them. Find a way to capture and store ideas as they come to you.

855. Buy a scanner. Scan appropriate material into files on your hard drive as soon as you find it.

856. Create a simple database. These are included as part of most office software packages. A database is invaluable to writers as a way to store material.

857. If you cannot use a computer, use a large legal-size accordion file, which can be purchased at any stationery supply store. Leave the file out on your desk where you see it often. When an idea occurs to you, write it on a pad. As soon as you are able, slip the note into the proper section.

858. When I interviewed Steve Allen, he told me he kept a number of small audio recording machines around him at all times. Find ways to grab those ideas!

859. Keep careful records, and cite your sources. This gives you credibility. Adapt it, don't adopt it! There can be a fine line between research and robbery of other people's material. Material in the public domain is available for you to use as you see fit. If the material has a copyright, you will need to gain permission to use it.

Create a Product by Taping Your Programs

860. After you are happy with the content of your program, tape your programs that are at least a half day long. Have the tapes transcribed onto a disk.

861. Use the live tape to create an audio tape album.

862. Use the live tape to create a CD-ROM.

863. Use the live tape to create a single audio tape.

864. From the transcription of the tapes, use a software program such as Microsoft Word. Create headings for each section of material. Word then uses these to create your table of contents and outlines. This will then be the basis for a book and the book proposal. You will find your book more than half done using this process. This material will also be your sales tool when seeking a publisher.

Recording: Sales and Royalty Rights

When your client wants to tape your session and sell audio or video tapes to attendees at the convention for a lower price than your materials, you have a dilemma. Associations often sell such tapes for $10 or $20. Of course, it is not the same highly edited material you sell as product, but it will certainly kill the sales of your higher-priced back-of-the-room package. If you are trying to get footage, allow them to tape.

865. Your speaking contract and fee schedule must stipulate that there will be no recording of your material by the client unless your separate recording rights contract is signed before the date of the program. There is of course a fee if they want to tape.

866. Never sign a release of all rights contract without a substantial fee or other value.

867. Go over the recording use and the recording rights contract as you negotiate your fees. This can give you additional bargaining power.

868.   Specify in your contract that the client's recordings will be for resale only at the _____ convention, etc., and not to be sold in any other way, or at any other time. (This is called first rights only.)

869.   List the right to record your program as an item on your fee schedule. Charge a set fee, or a royalty fee per unit, in exchange for the right to record your program.

870.   If you are going to allow clients to record, always specify in your contract that you are to receive the master and several copies of the tape of your performance.

871.   Bring several copies of your recording rights contract with you to the event in case you need them. Hand one to the recording people as you arrive.

Publishers

Many speakers swear self-publishing is the only way to fame and fortune; many swear by major publishers. I have many products done both ways.

872.   Once you have a workbook for your seminars and speeches, you can simply flesh it out and have your book and the basis for a book proposal to major publishers.

873.   Keep current with the news. Topics being sold on the newsstands and news Web sites are often the topics for which publishers want products.

874.   Keep checking Amazon.com's bestseller list to see which books are selling. Go to www.motivational-keynote-speakers.com and see the Resources for Best Seller Lists.

875.   Find product publishers that publish the kind of material you present. Go to Amazon.com and do a search for products similar to yours. Publishers are listed there.

876.   Write to appropriate publishers. Enclose a copy of your outline, three chapters, a table of contents, a list of competitive products, and your credentials with each query letter. You may or may not need the assistance of an agent when you approach publishers.

Self-Publishing

877. Sometimes a subject may be excellent for your speeches and seminars, but too narrow for a major publisher of books, audio, or video products. I created a *One Hand Typing and Keyboarding Manual,* and have done wonderfully well through self-publishing CDs and books and selling the rights for others to reproduce the manual. Many presenters publish many of their best-selling products themselves.

878. Read Dan Poynter's *The Self-Publishing Manual,* a self-published book that has done extremely well and is considered to be the bible on the subject.

879. Create your product yourself in small quantities. Make it the best you can on your budget.

What Can You Sell? Profitable Products and Materials

880. Sell the things you are already telling your listeners are valuable. The very best products for you to sell are the ones that are so obvious, you are most likely overlooking them! Do you talk on time management? Do you tell people they must have a special kind of calendar? What kind? Call the company that manufacturers them and set up a distributorship. Do you talk on leadership? Do you love to quote *The Art of War?* Then offer it for sale in your programs.

881. Create the product according to what you are telling people they need. Imagine in the best of all possible worlds what tool or reminder would help your audiences to use your information to change their actions and attitudes. Now go create or find that item for resale. One speaker, who tells her audience how important it is to smile while on the phone, offers a mirror with the word "smile" printed on it.

882. Write a book! Write at least one top nonfiction how-to book on your subject. The book you write will be the most valuable product you ever created.

883.   Sell books and products created by you or others:

884.   Workbooks

885.   Single audio tapes on each of your topics

886.   Audio albums that contain your speeches or related subjects

887. .   Video tapes

888.   Materials on computer disks, CDs, CD-ROMs, or floppy disks

889.   E-books

890.   Web online training

891.   Traditional books

892.   Software programs

893.   Articles

894.   Special reports

895.   Desktop reference guides—a job aid for details that participants aren't going to memorize anyway

896.   Task checklist pads

897.   Screensavers

898.   Speakers on time management, productivity, goal setting, or any related topic often create special calendars and appointment books or charts.

899.   Inspirational plaques and posters—often sold to clients for their many offices in quantity orders

900.   Sets of special quotes on cards

901.   Personality analysis tests that enable attendees to figure out what makes employees or customers tick

902.   Databases. As you develop information and contacts, consider ways to turn them into products.

903.   T-shirts

904.   Hats

905.   Jewelry with a message related to what you want people to remember

906.   Toys related to your message

907.   Join with other speakers in your field to produce anthologies and team products.

908.   Create generic and custom training materials for specific clients, for high consulting fees and continuing product income.

909.   Gather copies of articles you have had published on specific areas of your information.

910.   Put all of the items you feel attendees should have into a kit or bundle. You can save your audience members a great deal of time and effort and charge a great deal.

911.   Remember all of your services are also products. When you create a bundle, you can increase the value charged by adding an hour of your consulting time.

More Ways to Write for Profit

In addition to all of the ways I have mentioned so far to enhance your income using your skills, consider these:

912.   Become a ghost writer or cowriter.

913.   Become an editor.

914.   Articles you are paid to write

915.   Articles about you in traditional newspapers, magazines, and newsletters for promotional purposes

916.   Create a series of educational articles for your client's in-house magazine.

917.   Become a columnist.

Newsletters as Products

918.   Start a newsletter—print or electronic—aimed at your market, filled with valuable information to those it is sent to. If it is just a puff piece for yourself, it will be tossed.

919.   Publish several versions of your newsletter—some subscription-based, some not. One should be sent to clients you work with directly. Another can be sent to the speakers' bureaus who book you. A third might be sent to clients or speakers' bureaus you hope to work with soon. A few slight changes on your computer will enable you to do separate versions for your three or four target markets.

920.   Electronic newsletters sent via fax or e-mail are wonderfully inexpensive: no paper, no postage. They also arrive immediately instead of a few days after they were mailed. Most e-zines are deleted before being read. If you want yours to be read, it *must* have terrific information they can use today. Ask permission before you add anyone onto your e-zine! Your e-mail accounts and your Web sites can easily be deleted if anyone complains. Back up your list of subscribers each time before you e-mail your e-zine and 48 hours afterward.

Profit from Handouts, Workbooks, and Customization

921.   Always leave a handout or some other item behind with each participant with a small, nonintrusive mention with your contact information.

922.   You will create profit from the handouts and workbooks if you create them yourself and charge your customers. However, this is a great deal of extra work for you (printing, shipping, temporary warehousing). On the other hand, when your name is on it, you want the highest possible quality rather than a quick and cheap-looking set of papers barely held together by a staple in the corner, which is what most of your customers will do.

923.   If the client reproduces your handout, put on the first page of the master, "Reproduced under license by [client name]" so that if the client does a bad job of duplication, you don't get blamed for it.

924.   Add to your contract that the client has the right to copy your copyrighted materials for one-time use.

The extra copies are to be destroyed, the master returned to you.

925.   Always have your copyright at the bottom of each page, and the message "Do Not Duplicate Without Written Permission. Copyright [insert year] by [insert your name], and your phone number." It won't stop everyone from copying you, but it gets the honest people to ask first.

926.   To gain priceless knowledge and personalize additions, give the client the option of proofing the final draft.

927.   Always have about 10 percent more copies than the estimated number of attendees, but, just in case, know where the copy machine is and have an assistant at the ready!

How to Profit from Customizing Products

There is huge difference between simply personalizing a workbook and customizing your products:

- *Personalized* (custom cover with the name of the client): Your current materials simply rearranged and tailored with the appropriate modules needed need for this presentation.

- *Customized* (designed and written exclusively for the client): A highly customized workbook might have the client's own logo and buzzwords used, corporate philosophy, goals, objectives, internal policies and procedures, case studies based on job descriptions, work examples, and more. It is used specifically for a single client, and would not usable elsewhere. Products of this type command the highest prices, including consultation and writing fees.

928.   Offer to design a workbook, audio tapes, or other product that is so customized that it will not be marketable to others and will be extremely valuable to the customer.

929.   Place a value on the time it takes to create handouts, workbooks, and manuals when you quote your fees, whether you build it into the total fee charged or as an additional fee. Even personalizing an existing workbook for your customer takes at least three hours and sometimes up to several days. Highly customized materials can take weeks—even months—to develop. If you do not place a value on these products, neither will your customer.

930.   No matter whether you charge for each item you included or offer a package deal, use an itemized bill that spells out the high value of each item the customer will receive. Have the invoice say, "actual value," then the special negotiated fee you will be charging the customer. Use the difference between the two fees as a negotiating card for something you can barter.

931.   Create a workbook attendees would be expected to write in as you go through your presentation. These need to be a very valuable tool that you know they will refer back to in the future—perhaps where they have written their own lists, goals, and plans.

932.   Create a special reference booklet or handout for attendees to take home filled with information, copies of articles, and so on that they need to *use*.

933.   Suggest clients include customized audio tape material with the workbook that participants can listen to in their cars on the way to work. One way you can create these is by using existing tapped material and customizing the beginning and ending.

934.   Consider billing for one day to meet with clients and understand their needs, a second-day fee to develop the workbook, and then a charge per program participant for the materials.

Methods of Charging for Customization

Other than including costs for R&D in the speakers fee, there are many methods speakers use for normal customization and highly customized materials. The fees trainers and consultants charge for customizing workbooks and the products range from free, to cost only, to $50,000! There is no one standard that everyone uses. Use the following to develop the system that will work best for you and your customers.

935.   Charge a one-time design fee depending on the esti- mated time you think it will take you to design the material and the amount of intellectual property that you will be required to create (and give away forever).

936.   Charge a per-month design fee if the custom design work will be governed by a task committee that may be difficult to satisfy.

937.   Charge additional fees for attending out-of-town meetings.

938.   Charge for sending unusual amounts of overnight mail.

939.   Define revisions beforehand as any change not involving new design elements or new information, and allocate a charge for these.

940.   Charge for all revisions past the first.

941.   Bill per item, and charge from cost to $100 per item, depending on the perceived value of the item.

942.   Bill use of your product as a licensing fee, from a flat cost of $100 up into the thousands. A per-item cost is usually still added on, or you may allow customers to make the copies themselves.

943.   Bill a per-hour fee when clients are very unsure of what they need you to do. Per-hour fees are often billed in conjunction with other fees. These fees range from $50 to $2000 per hour.

944.   It is more beneficial to speaker and buyer when a per-day fee is used. It is easier on budgeting for the buyers, and easy for the speakers to estimate a quote for the R&D.

Ways to Sell More Products

Some like to call product sales that occur apart from your speaking "passive income." There is nothing passive about it! Major publisher or self-published, plan on promoting your products yourself if you want the book or other product to succeed.

945. When people buy a presenter, they are buying the hope that the new information given will change the listeners' actions and/or attitudes. While negotiations are under way to sell the speaker is the ideal time to sell more tools to help clients achieve their goals (i.e., the speaker's products)!

946. Be so good, interesting, and filled with information clients can use tomorrow that they will want to listen to your material again and again. This is where your products come into being.

947. Very gently remind your listeners they will only absorb and remember about 10 percent of most presentations. They will need to listen again to enhance their assimilation of the subject material into their lives. They can go over their notes, and you should encourage them to do so. But remind them you have provided a better way for them to do that in the form of your product(s).

948. Do an e-mailing to your own mailing list with special offers on your product and a free trip!

949. Include your product as part of your fee. This ensures a huge product order with every speech you give.

950. Sell product under your customers' educational materials budget, rather than the meeting budget.

951. Offer to sell your product(s) as registration premiums to increase attendance at conferences and conventions. Sometimes these gifts are given when the attendees register, sometimes at the door.

952. Always offer a quantity price for the buyer.

953. Think of alternative places to sell your products. Sixty percent of books are sold in grocery stores, drugstores, souvenir stores, tourist centers, and so on. What companies might be willing to buy your books by the dozen for resale?

954. Offer your product(s) as a premiums to be used by a company. Various premiums are often given away by large companies to purchasers of their product or services. Products purchased for premiums are usually sold in large quantities.

955.   Keep your eyes open for advertisements that come in your e-mail and mailbox. These are prime sources of companies that like to work with offering specials. Call their corporate offices and find out who set up their current promotions. Offer your product for their next one.

956.   Trade mailing and e-mailing lists of other topics that complement yours.

957.   Exchange ads or plugs with others who have newsletters and e-zines, and whose focus is complementary but noncompeting.

958.   Join newsgroups of those who might be interested in your topic. Answer questions on your topic, and have a brief mention of your product in your e-mail signature.

959.   Consider an infomercial. They are incredibly expensive to produce, but the profits involved can be equally incredible.

960.   Approach shopping channels to see if they will sell your products.

961.   Create a catalog with your own products, as well as other products that complement your own. This will be in electronic and printed formats.

962.   Put your catalog on your Web site.

963.   Add your link to your Web site catalog on all of your e-mail messages.

964.   Create an affiliate program that gives a commission to those who refer people to your online catalog.

965.   When you ship your products, include a promotion about your other products and services, offering some type of special. These are called bounceback offers. The offer might read: "As one of our valued buyers, you will receive a 15 percent discount on any of the items in the enclosed catalog." Or, "With an order of $100 or more from the catalog, we will send you a valuable gift."

Seminar Registration Giveaway Incentives

966. Use your product(s) as an incentive to increase registration for a meeting.

Back of the Room Sales Strategies

967. Please note that if the audience feels you are selling from the platform, you are not doing a good job! When your program material is good, people will want more. Audience members will only remember about 10 percent of what you said up there anyway! They will want something to help them remember and revisit your information if they like you.

968. People will normally buy the cheapest thing on your table. If the cheapest is $5, they buy that. If $50, they buy that. To create a $50 product, create a package or bundle of materials, rather than a single item.

969. Perfect your content to such a wonderful extent that the audience wants and feels they need to take more of you home.

970. Throughout your speech, make one or two subtle references to your products: "When I was writing my latest book on ____ (hold up your book), I discovered that ____ (set the book down again)." Or, "In my album (hold it up), I tell the story of ____. It illustrates the point of ____. Here is the story behind the story." Set the album down again. Then tell them what they want to know.

971. Refer to your sales table as "the autograph table." This technique creates a celebrity image.

972. Whenever you pick up your product on the platform, let your body language show that it is valuable.

973. Create a miniature bookstore in the back of the room, complete with signs.

974. Stack up your products so they make an attractive display.

975. Locate the autograph table between the exit door, the refreshment area, and the bathroom. Accessibility to heavy-traffic areas is vital for best sales.

976.   Bring a cash box, order forms, pens, and gifts for volunteers to your program.

977.   Estimate how many products you hope to sell, then ship them ahead to the venue before the event. A second-day carrier will see that they are there before you are.

978.   If you run out of a product at your autograph table, do not sell the last remaining sample. You can take orders and ship the products if you keep at least one set of samples to show.

979.   You must have sales table assistants to make change and handle sales. They will leave you free to sign autographs and talk with people who enjoyed your presentation. Rehearse your helpers.

980.   Let the introducer be your sales assistant. Include simple, brief material about your products in your written introduction.

981.   At the conclusion of your talk, have the introducer wind up with a conclusion that you have printed on the back of your introduction. For example, "Thank you so much! Our speaker will be available for questions at the back of the room at the autograph table. He has agreed to make some of his terrific books and albums available for us. The discounts offered are for today only, to this group."

982.   Give a gift to the introducer of one of your products. It's a truly appropriate gesture and gives you opportunity to briefly mention the book.

983.   Donate to charity a portion of the retail price of your products that are sold at the back of the room. This encourages people to buy.

984.   When you use an audience rating sheet, set up the reverse side as an order form. This saves time when attendees come to the table, and the technique helps you follow up after the event with those who are interested in more of your services or products.

985.   A prize drawing is a great way to increase the visibility of your products and to have the introducer talk about them. It is also an easy way to be sure you get your rating sheets returned.

986. Build a mailing list that includes the people who fill out your rating sheets. They are prime prospects for notification about new products and other programs.

987. Give a gift with order.

988. Back of the room sales must be done immediately after the presentation. If you encourage attendees to buy later, even after a break for lunch, your sales will fall drastically.

989. It is imperative that you get to the autograph table quickly when you finish your program. You court disaster if you do not do so.

990. Often you can set up a table where customers can fill in the entire order form themselves, including their credit card. The just hand them the product.

991. The ability to take credit cards as payment will dramatically increase your sales. Go to the bank and obtain credit card merchant status.

Sell Through Others' Catalogs

992. There are literally thousands of catalogs, online and off, that sell through the mail directly to the consumer. They are always looking for products to sell— why not yours? Promote your products to every catalog you can think of. Check with your library to find them.

993. Look on the Web for companies that have catalogs. Go to Google.com. Type in *books* [insert your topic, for example *leadership*], and *catalog*. Thousands of links will come up to companies that have catalogs that feature books on your topic.

994. Sell through online bookstores. Amazon.com and BarnesandNoble.com have made it very easy for self-published people to sell their items online.

995. Go to Google.com. Type in *books,* [insert your topic, for example *leadership*] and *amazon.com.* Thousands of links will come up to companies that already sell online through Amazon.com stores on your subject. Contact them and suggest they add your product(s) to their Amazon.com store.

Online Auction Houses

996.   Sell products on eBay.

997.   List them at other online auction sites.

Sell a Series

998.   Instead of selling things one at a time, offer to deliver one each month, or three each quarter, or whatever will best help participants learn and excel.

999.   This same idea can be applied to many things that complement your topic: flowers of the month, earrings of the month . . . you are limited only by your imagination.

Product Sales at Trade Shows

1000.   Trade shows offer seminars to attendees as a method to increase the value of the show to them. This can be very lucrative—a room full of your prime prospects eager to listen to your message for an hour or more.

1001.   Buying your own booth at a trade show can be expensive. Look for several others with related yet noncompeting products and/or services and cooperate on a booth purchase.

1002.   If you're speaking at an event connected with the show, negotiate for exhibit space. During your speech, point out that you'll be at your exhibit to answer questions, autograph your book, and provide other services.

1003.   Offer a small gift to bring the crowds: "Stop by our booth and mention you saw me, and you'll get . . ."

1004.   If you can do business with the show attendees, consider renting exhibit space. Only exhibit at shows your buyers attend.

1005.   Make sure your preshow promotion includes invitations to people you want to do business with.

1006.   Decide what one measurable thing must happen for you to call a trade show booth a success.

1007.   If attendees look at your booth and see a huge hodgepodge of many items, they will just walk away. They need to be able to understand with a glance just what you are selling.

1008.   Bring good staff with you that is aggressive in greeting visitors and quickly getting or giving them information.

1009.   Use a mike even in a small booth with two small speakers placed to the left and right of the booth. The speakers are hidden away and the volume is adjusted so there is no feedback.

1010.   If prospects seem interested, at least get them on your mailing list! Use a big fish bowl for a drawing. Encourage prospects to leave their business cards in it.

1011.   Walk the show floor looking for business.

1012.   Call prospects immediately after the show.

More Tips on Creating Income from Products

1013.   An autographed book is worth more than one that is not. (Ask any used book dealer.) Obtaining your autograph on your invaluable products increases the value to the purchasers.

1014.   Create a classy package that looks valuable.

1015.   Learn about international business practice before attempting product sales outside your own country. Bringing products into a foreign country for resale can often be a challenge in the customs office. Many speakers have been forced to leave all their products in customs and do their programs without them because they did not check on the restrictions before they left home.

1016.   All your products should act as advertisements for your other products. At the back of all your books, put an advertisement for your other products and seminars.

1017. Send catalogs out with each order.

1018. Include your products in all of your bios and fee schedules and on the back of your business cards.

Ways to Sell Your Products: Affiliate Online Programs

1019. In addition to other products, you can sell other services that offer you a commission. These are called affiliate programs.

1020. One very easy affiliate program, the easiest for speakers, is Amazon.com, for which you can easily create a page on your site that transfers people to a list of best-sellers on your subject at Amazon.com. You receive a commission, and your name becomes synonymous with these other more famous professionals.

1021. Look at other affiliate programs—for example, Radio Shack, plane and travel ticket sites, magazine subscription sales and literally thousands of others. First look at what you are already recommending to your listeners. Go to them and see if they already have an affiliate program set up. If they do not, check their competitors.

1022. Do not suggest services for which you are not already a fan, or which you have not carefully checked out.

1023. Create your own affiliate program, and encourage others to sell your products!

TOOLS OF THE TRADE FOR SPEAKERS, TRAINERS, AND CONSULTANTS

1024. To gain prestige and publicity, and to market your expert topics to those who pay for speeches, consulting, and seminars, you must have the right tools of the trade. To this end you will hear everyone in the speaking industry tell you that you must have a superb video and an expensive brochure to get started. Wrong! This is one of the tragic myths of the speaking industry. Only 15 percent of buyers actually hire speakers from video or audio; 55 percent are hired because of a recommendation from someone they trust. See "Cultivating Sales, Repeats, Spin-offs, and Referrals" in Chap. 3.

1025.   Get the right topic, the right market, the right business, and speaking skills. Without these, all of your promotional materials will be a waste.

1026.   After your career is beginning to bring you some decent and consistent bookings, I suggest at least 50 dates per year in the $1500 category. Do not create a video or an expensive brochure in your first few years in this industry. No one in any profession is at their best in their first few years. You will find yourself making drastic changes in content, style, culture, and even in the markets you will target during those first hundred speeches. It will be a waste of money to create expensive materials before then.

The Presentation: Your Best Marketing Tool

There are hundreds of books on speaking—I wrote three of them myself! I mention your presentation itself in this section because it is your best marketing tool.

1027.   Provide high-quality, industry-targeted, fun presentations at a reasonable price.

1028.   Be wonderful every time you speak. Underpromise and overdeliver your service, your quality of presentation and the amount of information you give.

1029.   Follow up with suggestions for expanded programs.

1030.   Do about one no-fee presentation a month.

Speech Tips for Higher-Paid Presentations

1031.   You are your best marketing piece!

1032.   Practice! Good speakers practice until they get it right. Superstar speakers practice until they *never* get it wrong.

1033. Create memorable trademark stories.

1034. To reach difficult audience members, focus energy and attention with audience members who are "with you" and obviously enjoying your message. That magic will spread to the others.

1035. You don't need to be a comedian, but you do need to find ways to incorporate fun.

1036. Invest in yourself by taking as many speaking classes, seminars, and coaching sessions as you can.

1037. If you do not have the money for coaching or classes, offer to help a speaker with back-of-the-room product sales or do office work in trade for what you need. Toastmasters has free classes and meetings.

1038. Study successful speakers: purchase books and cassette and video albums to hear the best speakers you can find. Try eBay if you are short on funds. You will find all of your favorites there for pennies on the dollar.

1039. Tape everything you do; take time to listen to the tapes and find ways to improve.

Look and Act the Part

1040. Be as professional as you can in your dress and manners and always be looking for the connection.

1041. Act like an expert, a speaker, a person with kind and compassionate answers to problems. The person you are rude to in the hallway might well be a prospective client, or a relative of one.

Topics and Titles that Sell

1042. Have something to say that you feel passionate about. Even if your topic is the most sellable in the world, your presentation of it will fail if you do not feel passionately about it.

1043. Although they rise and fall in popularity, motivational topics have consistently been in the top 10 best-selling topics for keynoters for decades.

1044.   For keynoters, seminar leaders, and trainers, some of the best-selling topics have always been: leadership, sales, motivation, change, humor, team building, customer service, strategic planning, technology, futurism, stress management, creativity, industry-specific topics, and goal setting.

1045.   Don't spend time preparing a subject that is only appropriate for people who do not gather together in meetings. Find the associations and corporations that need and want your topic.

Listen to the Marketplace

1046.   Have a message that your listeners perceive as adding value to their bottom line. It is a much harder road when you are the only one who perceives the value.

1047.   Listen to what the marketplace is asking for. If the programs you offer are only marginally relevant to the real demands of their jobs or the business, they are not going to be interested in using you.

1048.   Go directly to the industry you want to speak for and conduct a survey. Try for a cross section of management and workers. Ask them your questions orally or in a written survey. If you are doing the survey by phone, buy a tape recorder that will record phone conversations. Ask, "What bothers you most about your work?" (What hurts?) The answers are the seeds of a sellable topic!

1049.   "Find a problem, then look for a solution. Don't develop a solution, then spend your life searching for a problem for it. Pull through an idea from the market place, don't push it through from inception towards some intangible market."—Jack Ryan, inventor of the Hawk missiles, later known as the Marvel of Mattel, from Lilly Walters, *Secrets of Successful Speakers* (McGraw-Hill).

Ways to Get New Topic Ideas

1050.   Listen to people when they say "I need . . ."; "I have a problem . . ."; and "I wish I could find . . ."

1051. Check the best-seller lists constantly. Check the best-seller links at www.motivational-keynote-speakers.com to see what is hot today in your topic area.

1052. Record every one of your programs. Listen carefully to the questions the listeners ask you.

1053. Attend association trade show meetings related to your field and listen for topic ideas. Hear what is being asked about around the dinner table.

1054. Use rating sheets and add the question, "What do you wish I had helped you learn today?"

1055. Look at your subject backward. You might love dogs and want to talk about that. Not much money goes into that. But a great deal goes into the opposite. Who hates dogs? Those industries that need to deal with dogs in people's yards and pay millions out in workers compensation claims.

Tips for Producing Titles that Are Profitable

1056. Your title and topic must show the benefits to those who pay you.

1057. Put your target market group's name in the title. Every group is special.

1058. All titles must tell the listener, "How to ____, so you can ____." Start with this, then massage it into something quick and pithy. Write out the entire title, then take away all of the unnecessary words. Pare the title down to the very essence of the idea.

1059. Make the title easily remembered and repeated. The titles that are repeated often, are repeated because they are so easy that they can be repeated!

1060. Create titles that produce the image of sleeves rolled up and ready to go to work, not cute, complicated, or hard to understand. Titles aimed at the business world in particular should be straightforward and indicate a level of expertise.

1061. State the benefits to the buyer in the title—for example, "Increasing Productivity," "Memory Made Simple."

1062. Having a hard time finding your title? Check the best-sellers. See how they phrase titles and what catchphrase is selling today. Go to www.motivational-keynote-speakers.com. Use the links there to go to the best-sellers lists.

Designing Marketing Tools to Boost Your Income

1063. Before you begin, think of all the materials you hope to create (see later in this chapter). Design a theme so they to match each other in style, content, and color.

1064. As you look at your proposed design for a promotional item, ask yourself whether it *shows* rather than tells the prospect that:

- The audience likes you
- You are an expert on the topic the buyer wants
- You speak well

1065. Design your materials with the thought that the buyer may never look inside. Keep things simple and to the point. The front page must include:

- Your benefit-laden topic.
- Your name.
- A line or two of your qualifications on this particular subject.
- How the buyer can find you. (Actually, this does not need to go on the front, but it must appear on at least every other page: your address or contact info for the speakers' bureau that recommended you.)
- Your picture (for all non–e-mail and some faxable materials).

1066. The benefit-filled topic is the biggest thing on the front of your presentation folder. It is the reason buyers choose you. They buy your solution to their problem.

1067. A separate dedicated fax number, an e-mail number, and a Web site URL on a speaker's contact information give an immediate clue the speaker is a pro, or at least a real businessperson.

1068. Take a walk through your neighborhood supermarket and check out all of the sections, including the magazine rack. Look only at the colors and designs. When you see packages that attract your eye, you have a good ideas of the style you can use to create your own materials.

1069. Clearly show in your proposals and promotional materials exactly how the attendees will take your information and thereafter be better at a skill once they have completed your program. This is not something you will just say, but something your material must show has actually happened for past attendees. For example:

- Productivity increase by ____ at ____ corporation
- Profit/income increase by ____ at ____ corporation

1070. Produce your packages and the marketing tools in them in the minimum quantity possible for the need at hand. Likewise, use less expensive production options:

- Use two colors instead of four.
- Use audio instead of video demo tapes.
- Use customized color presentation folders from the stationery store instead of having a printer created customized folders or brochures for you.
- Print your promotional items in small quantities (20 to 50 at a time) on your own computer and printer.

1071. As you become more professional and your fees increase, your promotional materials must take on a higher-quality and more expensive image as well. You and your materials must look the part of excellence.

1072.   Never mail your full presentation kit to a speakers' bureau or prospective client without speaking to them first. It is disrespectful and a waste of money.

1073.   Never ask a prospective buyer or speakers' bureau to send back your kit if you are not booked. Asking for the kit back is just not the done thing.

Create Sendable, Flexible Materials

1074.   Create your materials to be sendable via e-mail, fax, print copy, and so on. This means you have a master on your laptop that you can click to fax or to change into a PDF.

1075.   Create a faxable version of your materials: no color, low dots per inch if you normally use a photo (or use a cartoon instead).

1076.   Be able to cut and paste information into a text-only format to put into the body of an e-mail. This means no fancy fonts or styles that can be used in other print media.

1077.   Create flexible materials on your laptop, which means you can customize the copy on your materials to match the potential buyer's exact objectives. For example, you might call the one-sheet program outline "Customer Service for Tellers in Hectic Traffic Areas," instead of simply "Front-Line Customer Service."

What Goes in Great Promotional Packages

1078.   Minimum requirements to include in your kits:

- The presentation folder
- A one-sheet content flyer on the topic which the buyer has asked for
- A letter on your attractive letterhead, and a business card (if this is not a bureau lead)
- A video and/or audio demo tape of your live presentation on the subject requested

- Your fee schedule
- A menu of the services you offer

More Good Ideas to Include in Your Kits

1079. Once you begin to be successful in the market, you will be able to customize the materials in your kit to be a smarter to fit your customers' needs:

- Lists of clients for whom you have spoken and/ or copies of letters of recommendation, and/or a sheet of testimonials with two- to three-sentence comments with the name of the buyer and the company
- A mail-back card addressed to you
- Biography information, often referred to as a *bio*
- Black-and-white glossy photos of you, taken both posed and while you are in action before an audience
- A copy of your contract (not needed when you send presentation kits to the media or to speakers' bureaus)
- Reprints of articles you have written on this topic
- Reprints of articles about you and your work, written by others
- Product(s) you have developed: your book(s) and/or book cover(s) and/or copies your newsletter if you have articles on a subject the buyer is looking for

1080. Have two versions of your materials printed, with and without your own contact information. The one without is for bureaus.

1081. Quality action photos of you speaking are wonderful for your promotional materials. Even though they are the very difficult to obtain, you need them. You need shots that capture you speaking and the crowd's response. This works very well if you work with a hands-free or long-cord microphone and are able to go down into the audience. Hire your own professional or a photography student, and/or bring your own camera and find a volunteer at all of your talks. Often they have a professional photographer at the event. Make a deal with the photographer to take extra photos of you.

Letterhead, Business Cards, and Postcards

1082. Create a card with your picture, your main area of expertise, and of course all the information on how to locate you.

1083. Create a novelty business card that people will keep. It must be either cute enough or useful enough that it will not be thrown away.

1084. Create customized postcards to match your business cards.

1085. Carry your customized postcards around with you. You will be able to fill time on airplanes by jotting thank-you notes to your buyers, bureaus, and those who have assisted you in your programs. A handwritten thank-you is always read and appreciated.

1086. Create your letterhead to match your business cards and presentation folder. In addition to your cover letter, many of your promotional items—fee schedules, one-sheets and endorsements—can be reproduced on your letterhead for a professional look.

1087. Less is better for content in your cover letters. Let the buyer know:

- The specific event these materials are referenced to

- What is included in the information package.

- A quick synopsis of what you understand the buyer's needs to be and how you can fill those needs

- When you (or your bureau) will be calling

One-Sheets! Most Important and Least Expensive Promotional Item

1088. The most important item you will need for the first several years of your speaking career is a one-sheet. Before you worry about the brochures and snazzy customized presentation folders, create an attractive content one-sheet for each topic for which you want to obtain bookings. It should be just what it sounds like: a single one-sided faxable and e-mailable sheet.

One-sheets tell the customer:

- What you are selling: seminars? Books? Dog grooming?
- Topic title
- Points you will cover in your program (short outline and/or bulleted points)
- Who this topic is most appropriate for
- A few endorsements
- A short bio stating why you are the leading expert on this subject
- What you look like (your photograph or a drawing of you)

1089.   People rarely keep flyers, but they often keep business cards. Print a synopsis version of each of your programs on a business-size card. This advertises the program and is easy for people to pass along or save in their card file.

Presentation Folders

Although Web sites have become by far more important, you will still need a good presentation folder. Top presentation folders often are printed in full color and sometimes have foil accents or elaborate die cuts. These high-quality types of presentation kits are both beautiful and expensive. The most popular presentation folder is printed on good-quality glossy card stock with pockets on the inside bottom. All of your marketing materials are then placed inside this folder.

1090.   Create your folder with a secure inside pocket so your items do not fall out on the floor. Some have flaps that are not connected. These will not do.

1091.   It is also a good idea to have a tab along the long side that extends to display your name and topic title when the package is placed in a file cabinet.

1092.   Consider adding an audio demo tape slot that can be cut on the other flap (or small crosscuts can be added to hold your business card). This makes it easy to take out your materials when you send them to speakers' bureaus.

Presentation Folders on a Budget

1093.   Your folder will be obsolete as soon as it is created, so create ones that are flexible, can be changed easily, and don't hurt as badly as you watch the trash man haul them off.

1094.   Go to a high-end stationery and office supply store or catalog company. These companies have many styles of ready-made deluxe presentation folders. Using these you can create your own customized folders in small quantities, customizing in many ways, such as using a label you can customize on your own computer; using gold or silver metallic pens; or gluing your business card, postcard, book, or product cover to the front.

Top Competitive Video and Audio Brochures

1095.   After you are making $3000 a talk, for at least 50 bookings, you will need a video demo tape. You will do better with a great audio demo than with a mediocre video. Use great audio demos first, then create a video demo as a means of raising your fee, not as a means to start yourself off.

1096.   Create your demo in many formats. Currently these include audio, CD, video, video clip at your Web site, or audio clip at your Web site.

1097.   Create demos in small quantities.

1098.   Create your demo with the first 30 seconds as your best segments. Don't waste time with an intro that contains flowers or graphics. They are not buying *you*. They are buying an audience on its feet applauding. Show that quickly. Total time of the demo should be from 20 minutes to an hour.

1099.   Prepare a separate tape for each of your topics. If you have four very separate topics, you must have four separate demo tapes (another good reason to use audio).

1100. Include in your demo tape vocal testimonials; a display of your products; a full presentation at the end of the tape; and your own credits and biographical information at the very end.

Rules for Creating Good Demos

1101. Your video demo must show you presenting at several different presentations. This creates the image of someone who is used at many meetings and is in demand.

1102. Buyers want your audio or video demo to be live, recorded in front of a real audience as you perform your speech on the topic they have asked for. Buyers do not like to listen to television and radio interviews, to see or hear marching bands or fancy swirls and designs. They want to see or hear you on the stage, speaking to live audiences.

1103. Listeners must see and/or hear the audiences. What they want from you is an audience learning and having a good time. Show this to them on the tape. Always make sure there are two mikes with a double feed—one on you, one on the audience. The way the audience's reactions will be recorded on the tape.

1104. While giving a speech, always repeat questions from the audience, otherwise they will not be heard on the tape.

1105. Never, *ever* use canned laughter!

1106. Remember to say at the end of the tape, "Please call the phone number on the front of this tape. I look forward to working with you to help you achieve your goals for this meeting." If a bureau has asked you to send out this tape, do not put your label on the front, put theirs.

1107. Select unique material for your demo. Never use a story that is well known or is not original. Bureau owners and buyers of speakers have heard all the old stories. Edit a section of one of your speeches where you give new material on your subject, and your audience is at its highest point for this first section.

Testimonials and Letters of Recommendation

1108.   Testimonials are a great way to create a word-of-mouth effect in print. Third-party endorsements from customers who are delighted with you are a terrific marketing tool. They give people a sense of security regarding you and your products and talent. You must use the name of the company and the person who gives you the testimonial.

1109.   Buyers will only give your materials a few minutes of time before they put them aside to look at someone else's presentation kit. So always customize your materials specifically for each buyer's needs, including testimonials you have received.

1110.   The easiest way to store your letters is to scan them into your computer. You are more easily able to use them as graphics in your other promotional material, and you can do searches by keyword to find the appropriate ones to send to customers.

How to Get Letters of Recommendation

1111.   Make it a habit to discuss a letter of recommendation with the buyer before each program. Explain that the letter is very important to your career and that you will especially appreciate the effort and thoughtfulness of the planner in giving it to you.

1112.   Help your buyers write the letter of recommendation. When you have finished a program, and someone important in the group gives you a sincere compliment, say, "I am so honored by your comments. Would it be acceptable if I quoted you in my materials?" When they say yes, make it easy for them. "Super. Let me drop you a note with that phrasing as you just said it." (Some speakers use recorders for this, asking first if they may record the comments.)

1113.   Use audience rating sheets each time you speak. If you get a good quote on one, call and ask for permission to reprint it.

Internet Marketing and Web Pages

1114.   Just as in any networking, be sure to introduce yourself immediately on your Web site: tell your visitors who you are, what you do, and how they can reach you. Give your phone number, fax number, and physical address, not just your e-mail address. Physical contact information makes you real and gives people options for getting in touch with you.

1115.   Put a video or audio clip up at your Web site for potential buyers to see or hear.

1116.   Have your downloadable biography available at your Web site.

1117.   Have separate photographs at your Web site for downloading. These must be at least 150 dpi.

1118.   Have free downloadable articles.

1119.   Have for-a-fee downloadable articles.

1120.   Include ways to easily see your expertise or special subjects, such as outlines and synopses of topics.

1121.   Include references and customer testimonials.

1122.   Clearly describe your style.

1123.   Have your current fee schedule, with all of your services and products listed.

1124.   The Web is not enough. Have a real person available who can tell potential buyers about you and your materials.

Additional Services to Offer from Your Web Site

1125.   Include your catalog with all your products and the products of others that will benefit your visitors. Use a shopping cart to expedite orders.

1126.   Have meetings for students in virtual classrooms.

1127.   Support request and response e-mail services.

1128.   Have a sign-up for your periodic e-zine (e-mailed newsletter).

1129.   Create 24-hour response to questions and constant accessibility to a network of trainers.

1130.   Create an additional Web site with no contact information, so bureaus will link their sites to yours.

1131.   Join affiliate programs that complement your area of expertise, and for which you will receive a commission, such as Amazon.com.

1132.   Create a subscription Web site, that people will pay a monthly fee to access. You will create tons of valuable information that would be very difficult for them to obtain elsewhere.

1133.   Get yourself listed in the online directories.

1134.   Create your own newsgroups or forums as a service to your customers. Go to your online service or your Internet search engine and do a search using, *create newsgroups*. You will find many articles that will explain how to create newsgroups within your own computer and Internet setup.

1135.   Sign your e-mail! Every day I get e-mail in which senders forget to add their signature at the end. e-mail automatically tells the receiver the e-mail address of the sender, but does not tell receivers who you are. All they see is your e-mail address. Something like "Loverboy@hotmail.com" is not very informative in a business communication!

1136.   Leave the address of your Web site on your voice mail so that clients and potential clients will have access to that information while you're on the road.

Marketing on the Internet

1137.   Write articles for other people's Web sites, making sure your URL is included in the article. You will be placed higher in search engines if your Web site is hyperlinked from many places on the Web.

1138.   Make sure the keywords your buyers will use to find you are in headings on your Web site. Many search engines use the heading format to determine how high they place you in the search engine. The higher up you are on the search engine, the better.

1139. Find someone outside of your business to sit down at a computer and explore your Web site—with you watching them. Ask them to think out loud and tape their comments. Do not offer them suggestions. You will learn dozens of income-enhancing ideas by simply noting everything they say as they travel through your information.

1140. Keep note of where people are going on your Web site by reading your Web logs. Ask your Web host, or Webmaster to show you how to view these. They will show you how many people come to your site and what they are viewing.

More Great Ideas for Your Promotional Kits

1141. Recycle the leftover flyers your client used to promote your speaking program. Rather than let them be thrown away, ask if you may have the leftovers after the event. Box them up and arrange for them to be shipped to your office. (Be sure to send a thank-you note.) Then use them in your promotion/presentation kits.

Remember

HOW DO YOU KEEP FROM GIVING UP?

1142. Have patience. It takes time to develop any business.

1143. Business goes in cycles. The slow times, too, shall pass.

1144. Believe in yourself. If your message has critically important value, then you need to be doing what you are doing.

1145. Remember the standing ovations, reread great client testimonials, and know that if bookings are slow it is not because of your talent but because of your marketing.

1146. Use fear as fuel to work even harder at marketing. Call all of your old customers. Network for leads.

1147. Have more than one pillar. When one area is slow, you will still have the others.

1148. Accept and use downtime. Relax and enjoy the free time. Consider new topics, write, and research.

1149. Work toward having a safety net of about three to four months in cash reserves.

1150. Focus. To guarantee success, keep your sight, hearing, smell, taste, touch (focus all senses) on your dreams.

1151. You must believe that giving up is not an option at any time.

1152. Read and remember the success stories of others in this industry. Many tell stories of living (eating and sleeping) in their cars while they kept working at success.

1153. Some of your best ideas will come out of fear and necessity.

1154. Take action daily!

1155. Think positive.

1156. Trust in a Higher Power. You must hear the call and follow it even through the darkness.

1157. Create a support team of others in the industry. Get on the phone and ask for moral support.

1158. It is better to do something for nothing than nothing for nothing. Go out and speak, train, and consult for free! Contact schools and non-profits. Allow your passion to overwhelm the worries of finances and low bookings.

PERSISTENCE AND TENACITY

1159. Be prepared to work very hard for five to seven years.

1160. Just do it! Don't wait for the phone to ring. Go to work in the morning and finish late in the afternoon.

LIFE AFTER SPEAKING, CONSULTING, AND TRAINING: WHAT'S THE NEXT STEP?

1161. If you are in this because you are following your passion, then life after this will be the afterlife. Extensive travel is the biggest reason for speakers to move on.

1162. The trick to not being on the road constantly is to speak less each year at higher average fees so that your gross income stays the same or goes up.

1163. Get passive income through royalties on products.

1164. Create a large company (with other speakers and trainers prepared by you and trained by you) to sell at the time of your retirement.

1165. Plan for retirement. Do proper investing and money management.

1166. Become an actor.

1167.   Become a recording artist.

1168.   Be a radio host.

1169.   Do voice-overs in commercials.

1170.   Write movie scripts.

1171.   Write your own TV show.

1172.   Work with youth and the underprivileged in developing their communication skills.

1173.   Advise new speakers and help them to learn the ropes.

1174.   Be more consultative rather than just doing a single event.

1175.   Go into teaching.

1176.   Get into telecoaching.

1177.   Create an infomercial that will allow you to sell large numbers of products. More product sales mean more stay-at-home time.

1178.   Don't try to predict the future; plan for it and make it happen.

1179.   If you are following your passion, then it will drive you to find ways to help, teach, and lead without the travel.

1180.   Finally, walk off the stage while the audience is applauding.

THE FUTURE OF THE PROFESSIONAL TRAINING, SPEAKING, AND CONSULTING WORLD

1181.   The owner of one of the largest speakers' bureaus in the world took it over from his father a few years ago. He told me that in the 1950s his father had been terrified that TV was going to destroy the speaking industry. People like to hear and see speakers and performers live who are interesting, informative, and entertaining and have that mysterious ability to communicate with their audiences and touch their hearts, minds, and souls. There will always be some form of speaking industry for you to work in.

HOLD THIS IN YOUR HEART

1182. Always give much more than buyers expect, more than you promised. Then, when they are pleased with what you have presented them with, give them a bonus. I told you I would give you 1001 ways—even at 1182, here is more . . .

BONUS CHECKLIST TO BE THE BEST PROFESSIONAL THEY EVER HIRED

This checklist will help you be better prepared in many ways. Many of the ideas are ways to help you increase publicity and professionalism. Sadly, in this latest version of the checklist, I have needed to include much more about your personal safety and that of your audience.

If Not You, Who?

Being the person in charge of others—a professional presenter, trainer, speaker, or teacher—is always exhilarating. On September 11, 2001, it became something more.

There were thousands of executives and public and professional presenters leading audiences that day. Then someone came up to them and said, "Excuse me, I need to make an announcement." Suddenly, the person in charge needed to be a leader of hearts that were breaking and minds in turmoil. Some rose to the task. Others just stood there too numb to act.

One audience, in a hotel at the base of the World Trade Center, rose en masse and ran toward the front doors. The speaker never said a word. Those front doors would have taken those people right into a hell of falling debris. Luckily, they were diverted to a safe exit by a fast-thinking meeting planner who was in the hallway.

God willing, none of us will ever have to face an emergency of that magnitude again. But there is no question that if you step to the dais, you are the one the audience will look to for leadership. Fires, floods, tornadoes, hurricanes, bomb threats, building collapses, accidents, robberies, and assaults can and will occur. During such times, telephone lines may be overloaded or damaged. Can you keep your audience safe if such a thing occurs? Do you know the fastest way to get emergency help to your group? Did you know using your cell phone delays the time it takes help to arrive? (Your cell phone will get you highway patrol, which takes all of your information, determines if there is a real emergency, and *then* forwards your call to the emergency agency assigned to your location. Now you start all over again. If you had picked up a land line phone and called 911, your call would have gone straight to the agency that would actually be responding, cutting response time by several minutes.

The speaker on the platform is in a privileged position. When disaster strikes, all eyes will go to you first. Do you have the answers? You will only have a few seconds to make your decisions before those hundreds of people in your audience all make decisions separately, chaos begins, and lives are endangered.

Most attendees run for the door from which they entered the room. People are crushed and exits blocked. No one notices the other exits to the room, because the person on the podium had not thought to point out those exits in the happy calm at the beginning of the program.

The advice offered here cannot be thought of as *the* way to handle an emergency. You, your insights, your tenacity, and your love of those you are trying to reach are the magic that is going to make the solutions you come up with on the spur of the moment the best possible in difficult situations.

Long Before You Arrive

Emergency Kit for Professional Speakers and Trainers

1183.   Take a basic first aid and CPR class.

1184.   Ask the hotel or management of the venue at which you are presenting about their emergency plans. Find out which disasters could occur in the area to which you are going. Ask how to prepare for each disaster. Ask how you would be warned of an emergency. Before 9/11/2001, most hotel staff members would be stumped by these questions; now they are better trained in these issues.

1185.   Call your emergency management office or American Red Cross chapter if the venue at which you are speaking cannot help you with emergency issues.

1186.   Ask the venue for an emergency exit map. Find a way to include this in your workbook or as an overhead. Although these maps are in every room, rarely will anyone look at them. Create a brief moment to review of them. Get your audience to focus on safety. Sometimes these maps are included at the venue's Web site. Hotel security might have them in the form of a PDF file they can e-mail to you weeks before the event.

1187.   Memorize basic emergency safety procedures for medical emergencies, fires, earthquakes, and tornadoes (see more later in this chapter).

1188.   Create and bring with you a kit of emergency supplies. There are two sets of things to include in your emergency kit: (1) items to help in case of an actual major disaster and (2) items for those problems that afflict speakers in most presentations: bulbs burning out, supplies not available, lights going out, and so on. Use the following list as a beginning to create your own emergency kit:

- Cell phone. (Your backup; use the venue phone first if possible to bring help more quickly. Never use your cell phone if there is bomb threat.)
- Flashlight.
- Tape.
- Scissors.
- Whistle.
- Aspirin.

- Compass.

- Waterproof matches.

- Small radio (consider a crank-up radio. They are small and cheap, and the batteries never run down).

- First aid kit. (Standard kits are available from drugstores and even some larger grocery stores.)

- Tissues (for crying).

- Extension cords.

- Chalk.

- Small can or tube of insect repellent.

- Anti-itch cream.

- Needle.

- Thread.

- Safety pins.

- I always carry a daytime hot tea flu remedy.

- Ladies should also remember feminine supplies.

- Your prescription medications.

- An extra pair of your prescription glasses.

- Credit cards and cash.

The Business Basics

1189.   Get it in writing! All arrangements, agreements, fees, and other terms should be written down, including how, when, and to whom to make payment. Carry copies of your correspondence and the contract with you in your briefcase or purse. If your meeting planner has been fired, you may have been replaced without notice. Be ready with proof.

1190.   Who pays for workbooks and handouts? Will pencils, pads, and other items be paid for by the hotel, the planner, or the presenter? Find out who will set the materials out and pay for the labor costs.

1191.   Get a deposit in advance. For overseas programs, get full payment in advance.

Professionalism

1192. Pack what you absolutely must have with you as a carry-on. There are only two kinds of luggage: carry-on and lost!

1193. Bring props with you. The meeting planner has thousands of details to attend to. Don't ask for difficult or hard-to-get props. If props *must* be used, design your presentation in such a way that you can carry them on the plane with you.

1194. Plan appropriate dress for the group. Check with the planner. The theme of the whole convention may be Western, but you may be speaking at a formal banquet. The presenter should always look businesslike and professional. Plan to dress slightly better than the audience, without being out of place. Never dress down. Look successful and elegant, not loud or ostentatious. Also check on the colors of the meeting room. Will your clothes clash with the site?

1195. The mind can accept only what the seat will endure. Find out what is on the program in the three hours before and after your presentation. Will the crowd need a stretch or a bathroom break before you can begin? Will people slip out before you are finished because they have another event in a different location? Work with the meeting planner in advance on the flow of the meeting. A receptive audience will take in the best you have to offer. Make suggestions on breaks to the planner to help make the meeting a success.

1196. Prepare a seating setup chart. Submit it to the planner several weeks before the event for approval. Also give a copy to the caterer catering a few days before the event (ask permission from the planner first). Always pack an extra copy or two.

1197. Let the planner know it's not effective to have the catering staff serve or clear while the presentation is in progress. Often the planner will forget to inform the caterer of this ahead of the event. Ask the planner's permission to speak with the catering people directly. They will need to plan to stop clearing even if they are not finished yet.

1198.   Get a map. Find out about alternative transportation in case the person who is to pick you up does not show. There are several places online where you can obtain driving directions. Try Yahoo! and select *maps*.

1199.   Who will pick you up at the airport? Have that person's home and work phone numbers and another emergency number. Be sure to take this information with you in your briefcase, not in your suitcase.

1200.   Who is the contact person when you arrive on site? Where will he or she be located? Often the main planner assigns someone else the task of "presenter sitting" once you arrive.

1201.   Send a copy of your introduction in advance. The planner or the introducer usually wants to practice before the event.

1202.   How many assistants do you need? Let the planner know.

1203.   Contact the assistant(s) if needed before you arrive to set up a rehearsal time. If it is difficult for the event planner to help you find assistants, go to your room early and ask the first people to arrive.

1204.   Request that the location and title of your presentation be printed on the program.

1205.   Request that signs be posted outside the presentation room door. Bring signs if your client does not have them. Get easels from the hotel. Attendees choose which breakout session to attend, and the presenter is judged by the number who do. Be sure they can find you!

1206.   Ship your materials to the bell captain. Call several days before the meeting to check that everything you sent is there. Use a second-day carrier. It's not as expensive as next day, yet still gets there quickly. If things get there earlier, they are often lost by the hotel.

Taping the Presentation

1207.   Arrange to have your presentation taped. Use a top-quality reproduction company if possible and affordable. These tapes can be used as demo tapes and products for resale. Only 1 in 10 will be good enough to use, so try to tape all your presentations. If the planner is not taping you, ask the hotel staff if the hotel has an audiovisual department that can do so. Often local colleges and universities will send out students to tape you at a low cost. (Murphy's Law for presenters is: "You never manage to tape your best presentations.")

1208.   Request two mikes, one on you and one on the audience. You want the tape to pick up the audience's responses.

1209.   Is the client taping? You are within your legal rights to refuse to allow planners to tape your presentation. You can require royalties or a reproduction fee. If you forget to check with the client about taping before you arrive, you can still refuse to perform, although your ethical rights will be in question for not being responsible enough to check before the event.

Publicity and Promotion

1210.   Write articles or press releases for the client's house publication and for industry magazines. This sets you up before the event as an industry authority and helps promote your image as a celebrity.

1211.   Brainstorm with the client's publicity or public relations team.

1212.   Negotiate for a publicity day with the client. The client may arrange interviews with TV, radio, and publications. You are paid an extra fee for the day.

1213.   Mention the host organization in all media coverage that the client helps you with. Also mention the event you are speaking at, your name, the location and time of the event, and your presentation title in any PR you do for that client or for publications that are distributed to those industries.

Know the Client

1214.   What are the client's special objectives and needs? What level of person are you addressing? Has the audience heard someone speak on your topic before? What were the good and bad aspects of that presenter?

1215.   Research current news about the industry. Check the papers, magazines, and TV. There are services available through libraries and universities that will provide you copies of all articles written on a specific topic.

1216.   Poll part or all of your audience ahead of the event. Learn people's specific needs, problems, and sensitive topic areas. Tailor your material to them. For example, if the audience is 90 percent female, do not use football stories. Speak in terms of their interests.

Double-Check All Details Before You Leave Home

1217.   Call your client no more than four days before the event to confirm everything. You will be amazed that even the state and date can change without anyone letting you know. One presenter arrived at the right place and time, but the wrong year. Another arrived at the hotel only to be told the meeting (out of country) had been canceled. Double-check the event location, addresses, and phone numbers at the site. Always confirm.

Delayed Travel

1218.   Book safe travel. It is your obligation when you accept a fee for your speaking services to arrive ready and refreshed at the site. Do not book yourself so tightly that you must take red-eye flights each night. Plan to arrive at least four hours before the event—preferably the day before. If your plane is delayed, you need the leeway to find alternative travel in case of cancellations or weather problems.

1219.   Find out who to contact if an emergency or delay occurs. If everyone is already at the event and your transportation is delayed, you need at least one other contact with the host organization to help get the message through to the right people. Call ahead to both the hotel and the planner.

1220.   Compile a list of several other presenters who speak on your subject. Professional presenters say the only reasons for no-shows are death (preferably yours) and natural disasters that would stop even Superman from reaching the meeting site. If either of these situations occurs, you or your next of kin should be prepared to have someone fill in. Some organizations require this standby preparation on the contract.

After You Arrive (Well Before the Presentation)

1221.   Let your contact know at once that you have arrived. Never let your client worry and wonder. You are there to help the meeting planner.

1222.   Make yourself known to the hotel's switchboard and message center people. Establish contact as soon as you arrive. Say something nice. Tell them you just wanted to say hello. Let them know you are expecting important calls and you want to thank them in advance.

1223.   Go to a hall phone and ask to be transferred to your own phone without giving your room number. Even after you have been there 30 minutes, the hotel staff still may not know you are registered there! Your meeting planner may call and become panicked, assuming you had plane trouble and are not going to make the meeting.

1224.   Double-check with the event planner to make sure of exactly which room you are to present in.

1225.   Check up on your presentation room. If it has not been set up yet, give the catering people the extra copy of the room setup chart you brought with you; they will no doubt have lost the original. If the room is set up, picture yourself as an audience member.

Go sit in the audience. Can the entire audience get the full benefit of your visuals with this seating arrangement? Will people be looking into the open windows behind you? If the room is not set up correctly, check with the planner. Sometimes it is impossible to adjust the room to your needs because the next group needs it set up another way. Try for a compromise, and offer to fix the room yourself.

1226. Ask the hotel people what the emergency procedures are. Each venue has different procedures for fires, earthquakes, medical emergencies, and so on. If you follow this checklist you will have called before and have an overview. Now you will walk through it all.

- Find the exits and actually walk the fire exit paths to the street. Never take elevators or attempt to force open stalled elevator doors in emergencies.
- Find the house phones. A land phone brings help quicker than a cell phone. Try to call 911 from the land phone. Often you will need dial other numbers first to make an outside call. Find out what these are. The only way to know for sure is to call 911, which by the way is against the law. However, if you are very quick in your 911 test call, the emergency services staff most likely will not mind. Your other option is simply call the venue operator in case of an emergency and ask them to call 911. You will have a huge delay while they figure out what to do.
- Find out where the closest fire extinguisher and fire alarm are.

1227. Pick two meeting places outside of the venue. Ask the hotel staff where two safe places might be. Most hotels now have emergency systems set up and will immediately be able to tell you. Actually go to these places yourself so you know how to get there and how to explain how to get there.

1228. Meet or find your assistants. If they are not provided by the coordinators of your event, find two from among your attendees.

1229.   Assign one of your assistants as the person to call for help in emergencies. Show your assistant where the phones are yourself so you are both clear on the location and what other numbers must be dialed to reach 911 emergency staff. *A land phone brings help more quickly than a cell phone!* Let your assistants know that when they call 911 they will need to:

- Describe the problem.
- Give the exact location.
- Give their name.

1230.   Be prepared for fire. Go over fire issues with your assistants.

- Always report a fire before attempting to extinguish it.
- Always keep your back to your escape route.
- Never attempt to extinguish a large fire.
- When using a fire extinguisher, remember the acronym PASS (pull, aim, squeeze, sweep).

1231.   Set up an emergency signal with your assistants. You need some kind of method they can use to let you know something is wrong when they don't yet want the whole room to know. When you see this signal, you will know to break the group into a discussion exercise so you can talk to your team. Only use this signal if you are sure your assistants know they have some time to spare.

1232.   Assign one of your assistants to get the fire extinguisher in case of a fire in your room. Walk this person to where the fire extinguisher is housed and discuss how it is pulled out of the wall and how it is used. I suggest a large, burly person—fire equipment can be heavy. Assign this person, or the one who is to go call for help, to activate the fire alarm.

1233.   Assign an assistant to be in charge of finding out the cause of loud noises. Tell your assistant to very carefully peek through a door. Tell the person to try to find a way to not allow him- or herself to be seen while finding out what is causing the noise. The chance it is a terrorist or other dangerous person is very slight. But why take the risk?

1234. Assign one of your assistants to check the weather report 30 minutes (or a more appropriate time, depending on your meeting) before the close of your event. Should inclement weather be an issue at the meeting location, you will want your attendees to have enough time to do what they need to do.

1235. Do a walk around your meeting room before the event. Find out if any possible problem causing loud noise might frighten your audience.

1236. Assign people to help you distribute your handouts in the quickest manner possible. Discuss exactly how and when this will be done. At meal functions, materials must be passed out after the dessert. In workshops, they can be waiting for attendees on their seats. Include the evaluation forms.

1237. Check camera angles if videotaping. While you look through the camera lens, have someone stand where you will be speaking and walk around as you do when you are speaking. Is anything in the background distracting to the viewer's eye? Will the lectern be in the way of the screen? Are unneeded chairs in the way? When you write on a flip chart or blackboard, is your back to the camera? Where are the dark spots? Stay in the light.

1238. Practice any prop moves, lighting changes, and other signals. Practice all moves alone or with your assistants, the light switch people, the introducer, or the projectionist, as needed. Appoint someone to each light switch. Practice your signals. Test your visuals in various dimmed lighting conditions.

1239. Practice adjusting the mike stand up to your height.

1240. Get all the electrical equipment up and running. Will you pull too much power when it all goes on and trip a circuit breaker?

1241. Bring extra bulbs and batteries. Pack them in your purse or briefcase. Do not leave them in your hotel room.

1242. Safely tape extension cords down.

1243. Write down the names and addresses of your assistants. Send thank-you notes and/or bring small gifts to present to them at the meeting. They will never forget you.

1244. Be sure you are spotlighted. Never work on stage in the dark. Some presenters carry their own spotlights and extension cords. You are the star, not the slides. Bring the lights up full as soon as possible. The audience needs only a few moments to review each slide. Then people need to see your face again, not a dark shadow. Double-check that your slides are in the right order and right side up before your presentation.

1245. Check the staging. What will the audience see directly behind you on the stage? A blank wall or drapes are ideal. (Moose heads should be removed—unless they are owned by your client.) Open windows must be free of sun glare—and the view of bikinis at the pool should be blocked.

1246. Unscrew the lights behind you. If there are wall lights directly behind where you will be standing, unscrew them. You don't want the audience trying to stare into a light bulb.

1247. Fix the seating if the house is light. Take the seats in the back away.

1248. Make sure your mike is working. Check the mike before the audience enters. Find out where static and squelch sounds occur, and avoid that part of the room. Cordless mikes are great. Many presenters bring their own. These mikes allow the presenter the freedom to move all over the auditorium in an arc as big as a football field. Some are handheld; others fasten on the presenter's clothing. But be sure to turn the equipment off when you are finished.

1249. Practice with your introducer. Bring an extra copy of your custom introduction (the one you sent usually will be lost). Give the introducer a gift—just a small remembrance to say thank you for doing a good job of getting the presentation off to a good start.

1250. Ask someone to time your presentation. Wear a watch with a very large face, or bring a clock to put just out of sight on the lectern. Don't go over your time limit. If you are forced to start late, check with the meeting planner. Are you to cut your presentation time down or give the full time? Adjust to what your client wants.

1251. Get pronunciations of names, titles, and current company status correct. Pronunciation is critical if you use stories that involve members or employees of the organization you are addressing. Print names on a card in bold black pen and tape the card to the lectern where you can glance at it easily.

1252. Post signs to divide the room into smoking (with ashtrays) and nonsmoking sections. Test air flow. Put the smokers downwind of the nonsmokers.

1253. Know where the facilities person will be at all times. You don't want to hunt if you're in trouble. One presenter discovered an error as she began her presentation. Her mike would not work, and the program from the adjoining room was piped into her room full blast.

1254. Where are the air conditioning controls? Remember, it gets a lot hotter when the room fills up with people. You should feel cool when you are in there alone.

1255. Ask the head of catering not to allow serving or clearing while you speak. Even if you have asked before, reconfirm about an hour before you go on.

1256. Do not drink alcohol. Many people may be offended. Even if you are drinking a soda, people will often assume it is mixed with alcohol. Consider carrying the bottle or can of your nonalcoholic beverage around with you when you mingle, and set it on the table with you at meals.

As the Audience Begins to Come In

1257. Speak with the audience members. Get a feeling for who you can "play" with.

1258.   Ask permission of your participants. If you plan on going over the edge with a member, take him or her aside privately and ask if this is OK.

Ten Minutes Before You Go On

1259.   Use the restroom.

1260.   Check that your water glass is in place.

1261.   Visually check that your props are in place.

1262.   Check with the event planners on what time they really want you to end your talk.

When You Step up to the Lectern

1263.   Smile.

1264.   Take a deep breath.

1265.   Look into several people's eyes and make contact.

1266.   Start your talk.

During the Presentation

1267.   Mention emergency procedures. If the MC or the announcer has not done so, casually mention the following to the group:

- "In the unlikely event of a fire, the fire exits are and ____. If smoke is coming from under those doors, don't use them."

- "Before opening the door, feel the door and/or knob. if either is hot, do not open the door. Open the doors slowly. If heat or heavy smoke is present, close the door and stay in the room."

- "Never take elevators in emergencies or attempt to force open stalled elevator doors."

- "If there is smoke in this room, stay down near the floor."

- "Open a window to let heat and smoke out and fresh air in."

- "Please notice if anyone next to you needs assistance in leaving the room."

1268. Tell your audience members where to meet if you need to leave the room. Ask that they try to meet you there, if it seems safe to do so.

1269. Ask your attendees to turn off their pagers and phones. Or have your assistant collect them and handle calls.

1270. Distribute your handouts in the quickest manner possible. At meal functions, handouts must be passed out after the dessert. In workshops, they can be waiting for attendees on their seats. Include the evaluation forms.

1271. Let the audience stand up to stretch at least every two hours. Every hour is better. In long sessions (over 1½ hours), include a participate section in which each member of the audience speaks to another, stands and shakes hands with a neighbor, and so on.

1272. Do not allow the catering staff to clear while you are speaking. Don't try to talk over a meal service. Make a joke and calmly, with a smile, ask the servers to leave. (Before you ask catering to leave the room, make sure the planner knew and agreed there would be no clearing going on during your presentation.)

1273. Remind the attendees several times to fill out the evaluation forms. Allow a few moments at the end of your presentation for people to fill out the forms before they leave for the next event.

1274. If you are taping, repeat the questions from the audience. Audience comments will not pick up well on the tape, even if the floor is miked, unless someone is walking a mike right up to the questioners.

Right After the Presentation

1275. Gather your materials. Don't forget to look under the lectern.

1276.   Ask for a copy of the tape. If the client made a tape, make sure you receive a personal copy.

After You Go Home

1277.   Send a thank-you. Send thank-you notes and/or bring small gifts to present at the meeting to the assistants who helped you. They will never forget you.

1278.   Never let your clients forget you. Send them news of new products and subjects that relate to their interests. Let them know you remember them.

1279.   When it's all over and everyone says, "I guess this sort of thing comes easily for you," just smile!

How to Recognize a Suspicious Parcel

The chances of a package or letter with something dangerous in it being left in your meeting room are very slight. On the other hand, are you willing bet the attendees' lives, or yours, that the package sitting on the side of the room is nothing at all?

Remember the procedures you need to follow on the checklist to ensure your assistants and hotel staff handle the situation safely, while your audience leaves the room in calm haste, with a bit of a laugh. None of that will happen on its own! Make sure you follow the steps in the checklist in the preceding section!

1280.   Do not go over and shake the package. Note if any of the characteristics in the following list are on the package. These will help determine the likelihood of the letter or package containing a bomb or a chemical or biological device. If any of the following describes the letter or package, then consider it to be highly suspect and potentially very dangerous and take steps to keep your audience safe.

Suspicious package or letter characteristics can come in the form of:

- Letters, books, or parcels of varying shapes, sizes, and colors.

- Take note if they are marked Foreign, Priority, or Special Delivery.

Return Address

- Address is prepared to ensure anonymity of the sender (homemade labels, cut-and-paste lettering), or there is no return address.
- The sender is unknown to anyone in your group.

Unusual Package Traits

- Audible noises (humming, ticking, etc.).
- Noticeable liquids; contents of package make a sloshing sound.
- Leaks an unknown powder or liquid.
- Emits a peculiar odor.
- Oily stains or discoloration.
- Excessive securing/binding material such as masking or electrical tape, strapping tape, string or twine.
- Appears to be disassembled or reglued; has a repackaged look.
- Has lopsided, unusually bulky, excessive, or uneven weight distribution.
- Envelope is rigid.
- Protruding wires, tinfoil, string, screws, or other metal parts.
- Misspelling of common words, especially verbs.
- Restrictive endorsements such as Confidential, Personal, To be Opened by Addressee Only.
- Visual distractions such as Fragile, Rush, Handle with Care.

Postage

- Postmarked from an area different than the return address

- Excessive postage, usually in the form of postage stamps
- Foreign mail, air mail, or special delivery

How and to Whom the Parcel Is Addressed

- Poorly typed or handwritten addresses
- Handwriting appears to be distorted or foreign
- Incorrect titles
- Titles but no names
- The addressee does not normally receive personal mail at the office

Excessive Weight

If some of the other items on this list are present, then you should never pick up package to see if it has excessive weight. If you pick it up and then realize it is suspicious, you've got a problem. I found nothing to say whether it would be better for you to gently put the package down or simply to hold it while you verbally tell your audience to leave and your assistants to go into the procedures you trained them in using before the meeting started. Hopefully, none of the us will find ourselves in that position. For myself, I would continue to hold the package while the audience went to the spot we talked about before the meeting and the assistants called 911—*Not from a cell phone.* After the room was cleared, I would put down the package.

What to Do with Suspicious Parcels

1281. Have an attitude that is resigned, lighthearted, but firm. Perhaps something like, "Ah, well, this is bound to be absolutely nothing, but we might as well stretch our legs and test emergency procedures."

DO NOT:

- Move or open the letter or package.
- Turn or shake the letter or package.

- Investigate the package too closely.
- Cover or insulate the package.
- Activate the fire alarm system.
- Turn light switches on or off.
- Make cell phone calls.
- Open, smell, taste, or squeeze the envelope, parcel, or contents.
- Pull or release any wire, string, or hook.
- Put the letter or parcel in water or near heat.
- Reenter the room until authorized to do so.

DO:

- Calmly ask your group if the package belongs to anyone. If it does not, and it seems suspicious . . .
- Calmly tell your people to move outside the building, perhaps to an outside location well away from the building to continue your session, which you would have mentioned in your opening remarks (see checklist).
- Calmly tell your audience members to
  –Take personal belongings with them.
  –Not use their cell phones.
  –Use stairs only, not elevators.
- As soon as your group is up and moving, tell your assistants to call 911 and venue management—*not with a cell phone.*
- Leave the room with your assistants.
- Leave doors open as you leave.

Glossary of Speaking Terms

This glossary serves two purposes: (1) to give you an idea of the definitions of some slang terms in the speaking and meeting industry, some of these are not yet in any dictionary, and (2) to give you a history of some of the words we use so freely from the platform—for example, *lectern, podium, rostrum,* and *enthusiasm.* Often I added the history of a word because it gave the word new meaning and life for me when I realized where that word came from. Often you can use a definition and history of a word to begin a presentation or to make a point.

English words often have more meanings per word than any other language. In this glossary I have included the meaning of the word or phrase as it applies to those who take the platform.

I am not a linguist or an expert in the field of word histories. However, I checked most of the words and phrases in this glossary against three sources (all of them against, at minimum, two out of three of the following):

1. *Random House Unabridged Dictionary,* second edition, CD-ROM Version, © 1993 by Random House.
2. *Funk & Wagnalls, Microlibrary 1.1,* © 1990–1992, by Inductell.

3. *Webster's Third New International Dictionary—Unabridged,* © 1976 G. & C. Merriam, Co.

Enjoy!

Accolade: Any award, honor, or praise. From Latin *ac-,* "at," and *collum,* "neck." in the sixteenth century an accolade was a ceremony that included an embrace to confer knighthood, sometimes done symbolically by tapping the sword on each shoulder. When a speaker receives accolades from audience members, it shows they are "embracing" his or her work.

Acronym: A word formed from the first letters or syllables of words, as IBM (from International Business Machines). (Note the difference between this and an acrostic). From Latin *acr-,* meaning "topmost" or "extreme," and *onyn* meaning "to combine."

Acrostic: A series of words, lines, verses, or other composition in which the first, last, or other particular letters when taken in order spell out a word or phrase. In the following example, FEAR is the acronym, False Evidence Appearing Real is the acrostic. From Latin *acr-,* meaning "topmost" or "extreme," and Greek *stichis* meaning "line," akin to "go to" and "stair."

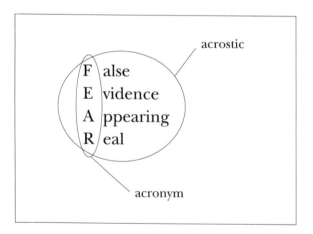

Address: 1. To speak to a group. 2. The speech or written statement itself. From Latin *drescer,* "to straighten or arrange things," to set in order. The archaic meaning was to give direction to aim. When you address a letter, you direct it to a certain party or place. When you address an audience, you direct your words toward the listeners, with the intent of their taking direction from the message.

Ad hominem: 1. When you direct your argument to your audience's personal feelings, emotions, or prejudices rather than intellect or reason. 2. When you attack an opponent's character rather than answering his or her argument. The ancient literal meaning was "to the man."

Adjunct: Something joined or added to another thing, but not essentially a part of it. For speakers, this refers to a thought added on. From Latin *adjunctus*, "joined to," "to join," "to yoke."

Ad-lib: To improvise something in a speech—perhaps words or gestures—that were not in the script. From Latin *ad libitum*, or "at pleasure." In music an *obbligato* is the Italian name for something you are "obliged" to play. The Latin *obligatus* ("bound") gives us the essential meaning (from Wildred Funk, *Word Origins and Their Romantic Stories*, New York, Bell, 1950, p. 297). When we ad-lib, we are not bound or obliged; we deliver at our pleasure (usually giving good measure of pleasure in return).

Agenda: A list of things to be done, especially a program of business at a meeting. *Agenda* is the plural of the Latin gerund *agendum*, and it is used today in the sense of "a plan or list of matters to be acted upon." *Agenda* is a singular noun; its plural is usually *agendas*. The singular *agendum*, meaning "an item on an agenda," is uncommon.

Amateur: One who speaks or practices his or her craft for the love of the craft rather than for pay. In Europe an amateur is often a gentleman: Prince Phillip is an amateur equestrian. In the U.S., where we tend to think of things in more monetary terms, an amateur is frequently perceived (often incorrectly) as a person with less skill.

Ambience: The special atmosphere, mood, character, quality, or tone created by a particular environment, especially of a social or cultural nature. From the French equivalent to *ambi*, "surrounding."

Amplify: To make larger, greater, or stronger; enlarge; extend. This can apply, for instance, to a speaker's comments, such as when more information is given, or to the method of increasing volume by use of a sound system.

Amuse: To occupy the audience in an agreeable, pleasing, or entertaining way. To cause them to laugh or smile by giving them pleasure. If you amuse your audience you are usually playful or humorous and please their fancy. The history of this term has me baffled. It comes from old French *muser*, "to stare." Does that mean in order to divert a person, you needed to have so much concentration on them and their needs that you needed to stare? Maybe the French got it from *Muse*, as in the nine daughters of Zeus and Mnemosyne who presided over various arts. I have often heard it said when you are inspired to speak, dance, write, etc., the muse has grabbed you. So it makes sense to me that *amuse* meant one of those Muses had grabbed you. This was what I was hoping to prove, but alas, it remains my own little unsubstantiated theory.

Analogy: A comparison between like traits of two things that are clearly unlike in kind, form, or appearance—such as a brain and a computer or the heart and a pump. From Latin *ana,* "according to" and *logos,* "proportion."

Anecdote: Anecdotes are short narratives, stories, yarns, or reminiscences of an interesting, amusing, or curious incident, often biographical and generally about human interest. From *an,* "not," *ek,* "out," and *dotos,* "given." Originally this referred to items not to be published or given out. We all know the best stories are those we are not supposed to tell!

Announcer: The person who makes announcements. We began using this in 1920–1925 in radio, and today we use it often in meetings. (Also see *Introducer, MC, Toastmaster.*)

Aphorism: A brief statement, tersely phrased, of a truth or opinion stating a general truth, astute observation, or principle. Also a proverb, adage, or maxim. For instance, "Power tends to corrupt, and absolute power corrupts absolutely" (Lord Acton). From Greek *apo,* "from" and *horizein,* "to divide." So you should obviously use an a aphorism when you want to make a point that divides the fluff from the facts and important stuff.

Apron: The part of a theater stage in front of the curtain.

Argument: 1. This is not just an angry discussion or quarrel. A speaker's "argument," like a lawyer's, is the reason or reasons offered for or against something. 2. Discourse intended to persuade or to convince. 3. A short summary of a piece of subject matter.

Articulate: Today we often say a speaker is articulate if he or she presented the case well with good logic. When used as a verb it also means it means to enunciate words well and distinctly. From Latin *articulare,* "to divide into joints," "to utter distinctly." Its original usage meant that something had a clear definition, as in clear segments or joints. For speech, it came to mean that something was clearly enunciated, with each part of the word clearly segmented.

Attendee: A person who is present at a meeting or event.

Attention: The act or faculty of attending, usually by directing the mind to an object or concept. From the Latin roots *tendere,* "stretch" and *attendere,* "stretch—to apply the mind to." When a speaker has the audience members' attention, he or she gets them to stretch their minds and thoughts towards him or her.

Audience: Those who hear your message, whether it is an assembly of listeners or those who are reached by a book, audio tape, television or radio program, and so on. From Latin *audire,* "to hear."

Audience participation: When the speaker has the audience do something other than listen to lecture—for example, discussions or games. Some will argue that when audience members are actively listening, they are participating.

Auditorium: A room occupied by the audience to hear the speaker. From Latin *audire,* "to hear," and *orius,* "a place for."

Autograph: An autograph is a signature written with one's own hand. From Greek *auto,* "self," and *graph,* "written."

Autograph table: Many speakers call the table on which they sell their products at the back of the room the autograph table.

A/V: Abbreviation for *audiovisual.* Refers to all the audio and visual requirements of an event, such as overhead projectors, tape recorders, video players, microphone needs, and so on. This term came into usage in 1935–1940. (See *Sound booth, Tech booth.*)

A/V booth, A/V area: Area of the meeting where the A/V is controlled. (See *Sound booth, Tech booth.*)

Back-of-room (BOR) sales: When the speaker sells books and other products at the back of the room, usually immediately after the speech.

Bandy words: A speaker who would bandy words with an audience member is hitting the words back and forth; a give and take. Bandy was a game played with a ball and racket.

Bio: Shortened form of *biography.* See *Biographical sheet.*

Biographical sheet: Usually referred to as the bio, curriculum vitae, CV, or vitae. Lists the speaker's credits and a brief history of his or her career. For speakers and presenters this is not a job resume. Length can be one paragraph—usually not longer than one double-spaced page.

Biography: A written history of a person's life. A speaker's biography is usually tailored to his or her experience in the topic area in which he or she is presenting. From Greek *bios,* "life," and *grapho,* "write."

Black and white: See *Glossy.*

Black humor: "A form of humor that regards human suffering as absurd rather than pitiable, or that considers human existence as ironic and pointless but somehow comic." (*Random House Unabridged Dictionary,* second edition, CD-ROM Version, © 1993 by Random House, Inc.)

Blocking: 1. The way you position yourself, your props, your lighting, and your equipment. 2. The path of action you take to move one spot to another on stage. If done well, it gives the greatest clarity of movement for the communication.

Blue humor: Risqué and naughty humor. As nearly as I can tell, back in the 1300s the meaning of *blue* was to be sick. But in the U.S. in the early 1800s, *blue* also became a slang adjective for being drunk, possibly because those who overindulge get a bit "blue around the edges." Hence "blue laws" to forbid drinking during certain days and times. Later that century, *blue* also came to mean risqué and naughty. My theory is that folks tend to get crude when they get drunk, their humor representative of their state of inebriation—maybe this is where we get the term *off-color.* Maybe too much black humor and too much blue humor will bruise the audience, leaving them black and blue. (OK, OK, it's weak.)

Bomb: In the U.S. in the 1960s *bomb* became a slang word meaning an absolute failure or a fiasco. The British also use it to mean an overwhelming success (go figure!).

Bombastic: All the definitions of this in my dictionaries were very negative—"a verbose grandiosity or pretentious inflation of language and style disproportionate to thought." (This seems rather bombastic if you ask me!). It means a user of language more elaborate than is justified or appropriate, perhaps language that's theatrical or stagy. *Bombast* or *bombase* was the cotton used to stuff or pad garments. It then came to mean a pretentious inflated style (kind of stuffy) of speech or writing; in other words, a "stuffed shirt."

Book: To reserve a date for a speaking engagement. The term originally meant to reserve something by entering it in a book of record.

Booking: The condition of being engaged to speak.

Bore: To weary yourself or other by dullness, as being long-winded. Once source says it comes from the Old English *bor auger,* which, more or less, meant a spear, a tool to go through something. Perhaps we use it as we do today because boring your audience is like wounding them.

Breakout Session/breakout: The splitting of the main group into smaller groups. A session at a convention or meeting where attendees are divided into several concurrent sessions to hear special material on differing special interest topics.

Brochure: A presenter's brochure usually lists speech titles, past speaking clients of importance, and quotes from clients and/or other famous people about the speaker. From the French *brocher,* "to stitch"—a brochure often being a few pages stitched together.

Bromide: 1. Not a common term in the U.S. any longer, but still used in some other countries loosely to mean a photo-quality original, mainly to be used for reproduction. (with the development of laser printers, terms like *bromide, velox,* and *slick*—all meaning a photo-quality original, will soon be only historical notations.) (See *Camera-ready.*) 2. A person or expression that is flat, dull, trite, and/or boring. Bromide is a chemical, a compound of bromine, that is used in film for black-and-white photography. The British chemist and inventor Sir Joseph Wilson Swan was famous for his work in photography and patented bromide paper in 1879. Copies of photographs were often made on this paper and became known as bromides. Today old photographs are still often referred to as bromides. *Bromide* as a slang for a bore comes from the fact that bromide was also used as a sedative.

Bureau: See *Speakers' bureau.*

Buyer: The person or group who signs the contract and pays for the speaker.

Byline: The line at the head of a news story, article, or the like in newspapers or magazines giving the name of the writer. This is an American term from the 1920s from the world of journalism. "Well! Where is the line saying who wrote the darn thing?" "The byline is right here, Chief!"

Camera-ready: A piece of material that is of a quality ready to be photographed for reproduction by a printing press, copy machine, or camera. Presenters are often asked to develop handouts and/or workbooks to supplement their talks and are asked to supply an original (the master image from which identical copies are produced) for event coordinators. Most coordinators request this master original to be camera ready so they will not need the piece typeset.

Over the years, many processes and systems were used for the preproduction composition of a camera-ready master, from an inscription engraved in stone to an illustration cut into a wood block or a text stored as digital information in a computer. In this century, once a master is made camera ready, many methods are employed to make a clear copy that can be used by a printer to make the duplications. With the development of the laser printer, this middle step of creating a clean, clear copy for the printer is taken care of by our personal computers and is fast becoming obsolete. Yet the terms still hang on, so don't be surprised when you are asked to submit an original and you hear words that reflect one of the many products or processes used to make those clear copies: *bromide, velox, PMT,* or *slick.* Today these words are usually a request for a camera-ready master.

Canned: For speakers, this has come to mean a standard speech or presentation. Originally it referred to music that was recorded and stored in a cylinder, rather than live. The myth is that if a speech is canned, audience members are left feeling they were listening to the same old thing, like a recording. This only happens when the speaker loses his or her enthusiasm for that same old speech and it shows to the audience.

Caricature: A representation ludicrously exaggerating and/or distorting of the peculiarities or defects of persons or things, to produce an

absurd effect. From Italian *caricare,* "to load, exaggerate, or distort."
(Also see *Characterization.*)

Characterization: Selecting physical mannerisms, tones of voice,
rhythm, and so on, for the creation and convincing and/or humorous representation of fictitious characters, or personas in your presentation. (Also see *Caricature.*)

Charlatan: A person who pretends to be more knowledgeable or skilled
at something than he or she is; an impostor; quack. From old French
ciarla, "chat or idle talk." Interestingly, *charlatan* is especially associated with those that offer idle chat. It comes from the old Italian
word, *cerretano,* meaning an inhabitant of Cerreto, a village near Spo-
leto. Its archaic meaning was "a baker of dubious remedies," which
just makes you wonder about the people of Cerreto.

Chautauqua circuit: "1. an annual educational meeting, originating in
this village (Chautauqua) in 1874, providing public lectures, concerts, and dramatic performances during the summer months, usually in an outdoor setting. 2. (usually l.c.) any similar assembly, esp.
one of a number meeting in a circuit of communities. *-adj.* 3. of or
pertaining to a system of education flourishing in the late 19th and
early 20th centuries, originating at Lake Chautauqua, New York."
(*Random House Unabridged Dictionary,* second edition, CD-ROM Version, © 1993 by Random House, Inc.) The Chautauqua circuit fol-
lowed the railroad lines and boasted such celebrities as Charles
Dickens, Ralph Waldo Emerson, Mark Twain, and P.T. Barnum. (Also
see *Circuit*).

Cheap laugh: 1. A laugh that anyone could get, because it is so obvious
or easy, like a sight gag. 2. An unkind, tasteless, or unsportsmanlike
laugh (as in "*cheap shot*"), preying on stereotypes or sexism: for example, saying to a woman, "Now clear your mind! . . . Oh? So quickly!"

Chestnut: Stories, jokes, or songs that have been overused and are stale.
From the 1880s. I found nobody who could tell me why we decided a
nut was a synonym for an old tired joke. One guess said, ". . . one plau-
sible explanation is that it comes from an old melodrama, *The Broken
Sword,* by William Dillion. In the play Captain Zavier is retelling, for
the umpteenth time, a story having to do with a cork tree. His listener
Pablo breaks in suddenly, correcting *cork tree* to *chestnut tree,* saying, 'I
should know as well as you having heard you tell the tale these twenty-
seven times.' Popularization of the term is attributed to the comedian
William Warren, who had played the role of Pablo many times." (from
Laurence Urdang, editor, *Picturesque Expressions: A Thematic Dictionary,*
second edition, Gale Research Co., Detroit, 1985.) My guess is that
chestnuts were very, very, common, so a common story got called a
chestnut.

Circuit: 1. A periodic journey from place to place. Usually considered to consist of several presentations at varying locations. 2. Just as it is referred to for a group of associated theaters presenting plays, films, etc., a single sponsor may set up a serious of engagements. The term was used by judges traveling to hold court, ministers to preach, or salespeople covering a route. For presenters, it is most often a reference to the old Chautauqua circuit days when speakers were sent around the country on a speaking circuit or tour. (Also see *Chautauqua circuit.*)

Classroom-style seating: When the seating for the audience is set up with tables in front of seats.

Cliché: A trite, stereotyped expression, sentence, or phrase. Originally a printing press used wooden blocks (later metal was used to cope with the stress of bigger runs) called clichés or stereotypes. Since a cliché is used over and over, some clever person used the word to mean an expression that is used over and over.

Client: Whoever is paying for the service. A company or association is the client when they buy the speaker. A speaker may be the client of an agent who is paid or receives a commission of earnings to manage the speaker.

Clique: Any small, exclusive, clannish group of people. In an audience, attendees tend to form in or associate in cliques. The learning level in training and seminar settings is considered to be higher if attendees are broken out of the cliques they arrived in. From the 1700s, possibly a likening of Middle French *clique*, "latch."

Close to the edge: See *Edge.*

Community service speakers' bureau: A speakers' bureau that sends presenters into a community or industry, usually at little or no cost, to speak on topics that promote the sponsoring company or on public awareness issues.

Compassion: Deep sympathy for the needs of another with the desire to help or spare. From Latin *com*, "together" and *pati*, "to feel." As a speaker, you attempt to bring your own feelings for others together with their feelings and needs.

Conclude: To bring to an end; finish; terminate. From Latin *com*, "thoroughly" and *claudere*, "to close, shut off."

Concluder: In a speech, the final remarks given to finish the presentation. A concluder could be used by the speaker to close a presentation, but it also refers to the remarks the MC or announcer makes to conclude that particular session.

Concurrent (sessions): Concurrent or breakout sessions. (See *Breakout.*)

Connection: The bonding, association, or relationship of the presenter with the audience's emotions.

Consult: To seek advice, guidance, or information from someone. Refers to giving or asking of advice. From Latin *consulere,* "to seek advice."

Consultant: Person who gives professional or technical advice. Speakers often consult with clients to prepare customized material for programs or workbooks for an added fee. An example might be an expert who sits in on telephone complaint calls in order to prepare material for workshops to train employees in handling problem customers. The term came in usage in the late 1600s.

Content: That which a thing contains, such as the contents of a box— in our case, the subject matter. For example, "We want a speaker with content!", meaning audiences want speakers with usable data and ideas they can apply to their own situations, rather than "fluff."

Contract: A formal legal instrument used to state agreement between speaker and client and/or bureau. Details the exact terms of payment and performance.

Convey: To communicate; transmit; make known: from Latin *com,* "together" and *via,* "road or way." When we teach, we use the roadway of words to bring together the mind of the speaker and that of the listener.

Cordless: Slang for cordless microphone; wireless mike. A cordless could be a handheld or a lavaliere.

Curriculum vitae: Also called just plain *vitae* or *CV.* A brief biographical resume of the presenter's career and training. This term is most commonly used by the academic community. See *Biographical sketch.*

CV: See *Biographical sketch, Curriculum vitae, Vitae.*

Dais: A raised platform, as at the front of a room where the speaker presents from. Also called platform, podium, riser, or stage. From Latin *discus,* "table."

Deadpan: A completely expressionless face, and a style of comedic technique that uses a completely expressionless face. U.S. slang from the 1920s. "*Pan* has been used since at least the early 19th century to mean 'the face,' possibly because the face is 'broad, shallow and often open,' as *Webster's* suggests, but just as likely because pan meant 'the skull or head' as far back as the early 14th century and was used by Chaucer." (From Robert Hendrickson, *Encyclopedia of Word and Phrase Origins,*" p. 153–154.)

Demo: Audio or visual demonstration tapes. Used to promote speakers' services or speeches to buyers.

Desultory: Jumping from one thing to another; unmethodical, random. Roman acrobats who would jump from one fast-moving horse to another were called *desultores* (leapers). If you deliver a speech in a desultory fashion, you leap from one thought to another.

Digress: When a speaker steps away from the main subject, he or she digresses, or rambles and wanders around the presentation—not a pretty picture. From Latin *di*, "away, apart" and *gradi*, "to go, step."

Discourse: To send forth one's ideas concerning a subject, communication of thought by words; talk; conversation. From Latin *dis*, "apart" and *cursus*, "running."

Discuss: To have as the subject of conversation or writing; especially to explore solutions. From Latin *discutere*, "to discuss," *dis*, "apart" and *guatere*, "to shake." Interesting, as a speaker when you allow them to discuss, they are shaken apart with understanding? Maybe so!

Downstage: At or toward the front of the stage. In olden days, a theatre was often down in a small ravine. The audience was on one hillside, the stage on the other. Downstage was the point that was the farthest down the hill; upstage was the point farthest up the stage or up the hill. (See *Upstage*.) This made it easier for the audience to see and hear. Even today a speaker will say, "Come on down here with me!" meaning "Come downstage to where I am."

Dyad: A group of two; couple; pair.

Dynamic: When a presentation seems to be filled with energy and/or effective action and forcefulness: from Greek *dynamis*, "power."

Easel: A folding frame or tripod used to support the flip charts and the like. In Dutch a donkey is called an *ezel*. A donkey is wonderfully patient assistant that bears its burden without complaint for hours—hence the artist's *ezel* would hold its burden. Today a speaker has this same faithful friend in most meetings. (Also see *Flip chart*.)

Edge: This came into usage in the early 1900s. When you reach the limit, then go past it, you've gone over the edge. The extreme of what is expected and/or acceptable to your listener. Hence the expressions *over the edge, close to the edge, on the edge*. A humorist may have the audience rolling on the floor with mildly racy humor (close to the edge), but if he or she steps too far over the edge, that is when the audience starts to think, "that's not funny, it's just plain dirty/gross/etc.!" The challenge to any presenter is discovering where this undefined edge is for you and your audience.

Elocution: The art, study, and practice of public speaking or reading aloud in public, including vocal delivery and gesture. Also refers to your manner of speaking.

Elocutionist: Someone adept at elocution—public speaking and voice production. An older term, not widely used anymore. From Latin *e*, "out" and *loqui*, "to speak."

Eloquent/eloquence: A speaker who uses expressiveness; the fluent, polished, and effective use of language. The quality of speaking in a moving, forceful, or persuasive way. From Latin *e*, "out" and *loqui*, "to speak."

Emcee: Informal way of referring to the master of ceremonies at a banquet; often spelled MC. Also see *Announcer, Introducer, Master of Ceremonies, MC,* and *Toastmaster.*

Emotion: "A strong surge of feeling marked by an impulse to outward expression and often accompanied by complex bodily reactions; any strong feeling, as love, hate, or joy." (*Funk & Wagnalls Microlibrary 1.1,* © 1990–1992, by Inductell) From the Latin *emotio* and *onis; e*, "out" and *movere*, "to move." This is where the expression "to move an audience" (when we have "touched their emotions") undoubtedly comes from.

Energetic: One has or exhibits energy when one is powerful in action or effectiveness. From the Greek *en-* and *ergon*, "work." Interestingly, being energetic on the platform can only be achieved by hard work.

E-news: Electronic newsletter sent via e-mail. (See *e-zine.*)

Enjoy: To experience with joy; take pleasure in. From the 1350s Middle English *enjoyen*, "to make joyful," which in turn comes from the Old French *enjoier*, "to give joy to." It is rather a lovely moral message to realize both roots involve the giving of joy. Perhaps the old guys were wiser than us to know that to get it, you must give it first.

Enthusiasm: 1. A keen, animated interest; an absorbing or controlling possession of the mind by any subject, interest, or pursuit. From Greek *entheos, enthous*, "inspired, possessed." Originally this meant people who in religious situations seemed so inspired as to be possessed by God (*theos*). The expression has almost lost its religious meaning. 2. A passionate elevation of soul. We speakers have all felt the wonderful filling up with spirit that happens when we are speaking well, then the joy as that spirit pours from us into our audience and they become filled with enthusiasm—as if filled with god's spirit.

Enunciate: To pronounce words distinctly in an articulate or a particular way. From Latin *e*, "out" and *nuntiare*, "to announce."

Eulogize: Although often thought of as the address given at a funeral, it actually means to extol and laud, either through speaking or writing a eulogy, a piece of high praise. From Greek *eu*, "well" and *legein*, "to speak."

Expatiate: To elaborate at length with copious descriptions or discussion. From Latin *ex*, "out" and *spatiari*, "to wander about." The archaic meaning was to intellectually and imaginatively move around.

Experiential exercise: Audience participation exercise where the lessons learned are derived from experience used to convey the lesson. For example, when you touch the hot stove when you are young, you have just learned a lesson via an experiential learning method. (Also see *audience Participation.*)

Expostulate: To reason earnestly with a person against something he or she is inclined to do. The term came into use in the 1520s. From Latin *expostulatus*, "demanded urgently, required."

Extemporaneous: Prepared with regard to content but not read or memorized word for word. From Latin *ex*, "out" and *tempus, temporis*, "time."

E-zine: Electronic magazine or newsletter. (See *e-news*.)

Flip chart: A chart with pieces of paper, usually set on an easel. Used by the speaker to clarify points. Also see *Easel*.

Flippant: Remarks given without enough forethought, often characterized by levity.

Flop: To be completely unsuccessful. The entire talk may be a flop, or just a portion—a joke, anecdote and so on. From the late 1890s.

Flop sweat: 1. Fear of performing. 2. Actual perspiration when fearful of performing.

Fluent: Capable of speaking or writing with effortless ease as in running freely like a stream of water. From the Latin *fluens, fluere*, "to flow."

Flyer: A one-sheet piece of printed advertising, letter or legal size. Often produced to promote the presenter's program, products, or services.

Focus: The concept or ideas on which the mind is concentrated and centered. From the 1630s, from the Latin word for *fireplace*. The Romans had their fireplace as the center of their family life. The root of this same word came to mean the central point for our interest; it has a similar meaning in optics, physics, and geometry. In one of his books, Norman Vincent Peale's comments seem to tie fire and focus together: "Walt Whitman said of himself, 'I was simmering, really simmering; Emerson brought me to a boil.' What an apt description of a personality, gifted but lacking in power until the fire of enthusiasm brought it to a the boiling point."

Foil: 1. A person or thing that makes another seem better by contrast. This person could be, but is not necessarily, a "plant." (See *Plant*.) When the foil stops being a good contrast for the presenter, he or she would then be categorized as a heckler (See *Heckler*.) 2. Term used for overhead slide transparencies—more commonly used in aerospace or high-tech companies and in Europe. The term seems to be based on an older method of making overheads from the 1950s when the overhead was produced on foil-like material. Any metal in the form of very thin sheets is referred to as *foil*. From the Latin *folium*, "leaf." Later, in Old French, *foil* came to mean to decorate with leaflike designs, often in thin metals.

Forte: A person's strong point, something in which he or she excels. "He is a humorist, but magic is his forte." A two-syllable pronunciation (FOR-tay) is often heard, perhaps confusing this word with the musical term *forte,* which similarly means loudly and forcefully. The historical pronunciation of *forte* is one syllable (FORT). Both pronunciations are correct. The word is derived from French *fort,* "strong."

Fulminate: As when something, such as a chemical, explodes suddenly and violently, a speaker fulminates when he or she makes loud or violent denunciations or scathing verbal attacks, or when giving a scathing rebuke or condemnation. From Latin *fulmen, fulminis,* "lightning."

Gab: To talk, chatter, yak, rap, schmooze, or chat idly. *Funk & Wagnalls* thinks it is probably from Old Norse *gabba,* "to mock." But *Random House* feels it perhaps comes from the 1540–1550 Scottish Gaelic *gob,* "mouth." Even old French *gobe* means "mouthful." When you have the "gift of gab," you are gifted with the use of your mouth.

Gag: A joke or any built-in piece of wordplay or horseplay. It comes from the theatre. Historians seemed to be puzzled by its origin. Some speculate it might have meant that a jokester would finally annoy his audience so badly they would want to gag him.

Garble: To mix up, jumble, or confuse, facts, ideas, stories, and so on unintentionally or ignorantly. From Arabic *gharbala,* "to sift or purify." "But by the seventeenth century it had come to mean 'sifting' information maliciously—putting together selected bits to distort the meaning. Nowadays, the malice has dropped out, and the information is merely muddled." (From Robert Claiborne, *Loose Cannons and Red Herrings,* Ballantine Books, 1980, p. 111.)

General assembly: A gathering of all attendees at a meeting or convention; usually implies a session other than a meal function. A general assembly often, but certainly not always, follows a meal session, in the same room because everyone is already sitting in that location.

Genre: A class or category of artistic endeavor having a particular form, content, technique, or the like. The term came into usage in the mid 1750s and can be traced to Latin *genus,* "race or kind," the same root we get *gender* from.

Gesticulate: To use emphatic or expressive gestures, especially in an animated or excited manner. From Latin *gesticulus,* diminutive of *gestus,* which is where we get the word *gesture.*

Gig: Slang term for booking or engagement.

Glib: When you speak fluently but without much thought, you are a glib talker. More superficial than sincere. From Middle Low German *glibberich,* "slippery."

Glossary: A list of terms in a special subject area, explaining the technical, obscure, difficult or unusual words and expressions used, or a list of the same at the back of a book, explaining or defining these. From Greek *gloss-*, "tongue." It's easy to see how it came mean a collection of words with which the tongue might have trouble.

Glossy: Slang for a glossy photograph. Usually refers to a black-and-white promotional photograph of the presenter. Also called a black and white or B&W.

Greenroom: Room backstage in a theater, broadcasting studio, or the like, where speakers can relax when they are not on stage or on camera. Random House's dictionary dates its usage from the late 1600s. The real reason we call it a greenroom is lost to antiquity. One drama friend of mine recalls a possible fable in connection with the with the Globe Theatre in England. The actors performing in Shakespeare's open-air theater had to face the summer sun all afternoon, so the legend has it that the actors' resting space backstage was painted green as a restorative to the eyes. Another says the terrible glare from the limelights was so harsh that the actors needed a dark place to rest after a show—hence a room painted dark green. The *Encyclopedia of Word and Phrase Origins,* by Robert Hendrickson (p. 234, *Facts on File,* New York © 1987) says, "... probably takes its name from such a room in London's Durry Lane Theatre, which just happened to be painted green sometime in the late 17th century. Most authorities reject the old story that the room was painted green to soothe the actors' eyes." Note that this is 100 years later than Random House cites, but it first appears in print in 1678, so maybe Random House is right. The *Oxford Companion to the Theater* also thinks it is most probably is called the greenroom because it was originally painted green, but also notes that "It was also known as the Scene Room, a term later applied to a room where scenery was stored, and it has been suggested that 'green' is a corruption of 'scene' " (Phyllis Hartnaoll, *The Oxford Companion to the Theater,* fourth edition, Oxford University Press, Oxford, 1983, p. 352). So, only the ghosts of actors past know the truth about the greenroom.

Gross fee: The total fee the buyer is charged for a booking, including agents' fees and excluding expenses.

Hack writer: One who hires out his or her services to write—especially for routine work. It often means the writing is stale or trite by constant use. A hack was a horse for hire (today in the U.S. a taxicab a is hack). These horses were often thought of as old and wornout.

Ham: A presenter or an actor who overacts or exaggerates. The history of this term is varied. Possibly from actors that were of the lower order who removed their makeup with inexpensive ham fat. However, according to my Random House Unabridged dictionary, "1880–85; short for hamfatter, after 'The Hamfat Man,' a black minstrel song." Finally, my nephew Michael thinks it is because a presenter tends to "hog" the limelight, so is a ham.

Handheld: Slang for a handheld microphone. A handheld comes in a cord or cordless version.

Handout: Informative or educational material given to the audience. Often in flyer form, but refers to anything that is handed out to the audience.

Hands-free mike: Microphone that attaches to the speaker's clothing.

Harangue: A lengthy, loud, and vehement speech; tirade. From Old High German *hari,* "army, host" and *hringa,* "ring."

Head table: Table at the front of the room. Reserved for the key people at a meeting.

Heart story: A story that touches the heart, spirit, or soul of the listener. These are usually thought of as those vignettes that bring a tear to the eye.

Heckle: To annoy the presenter with taunts, questions, and so on. "The original verb meant to straighten and disentangle the fibers of flax or hemp, by drawing them through a heavy, sharp-toothed iron comb; later it took on the additional meaning of "scratch." A speaker who's being severely heckled may well feel as if he's being scratched with such a comb." (From Robert Claiborne, *Loose Cannons and Red Herrings,* Ballantine, 1980, p. 130.)

Heightening: Intensifying the audience's or the presenter's awareness, sensitivity, or understanding of a subject. Presenters heighten themselves when their presentation creates a greater enthusiasm and or a greater dimension through their connection to the audience. The audience members are heightened if the connection is made and understanding and enlightenment dawn in their minds.

Hem and haw: When you are at a loss for words, so you say things that really are not saying much of anything—for example, "Well, uh, you see, um, I was just . . . well, I had thought that. . . . uh." From the sixteenth century.

Hoarse: A husky, gruff, or croaking voice, deep, harsh, and grating in sound.

Honorarium: Payment given to a speaker. Usually refers to politicians and others in industries where payment for speaking forbids a set fee.

House: Slang expression for the building in which you are speaking, or for the number of attendees in the building. "How's the house?" means how many audience members are sitting in the venue. "The house is dim" means the room is lighted poorly.

House lights: The lights that illuminate the audience rather than the stage.

Humor: The quality of anything that is funny or appeals to the comic sense. From Latin *umere,* "to be moist." Today it means The quality of anything that is funny or appeals to the comic sense. In ancient physiology it referred to one of the four principal bodily fluids (cardinal humors): blood, phlegm, choler (yellow bile), and melancholy (black bile), which were believed to influence health and temperament according to their proportions in the body.

Idiom: 1. An expression peculiar to a language, not readily understandable from the meaning of its parts; an expression whose meaning is not predictable from the usual meanings of its constituent elements. Examples are "to put up with," "kick the bucket," or "hang one's head." 2. A language, dialect, or style of speaking peculiar to a people or region. 3. The special terminology of an industry, class, occupational group, and so on. From Greek *idios,* "one's own."

Impresario: A producer or director of rallies or programs for the public, operas, concerts, or musical comedies. Programs organized by impresarios for speakers are usually in large sports arenas or auditoriums.

Improve: From Old French *en,* "into" and *prou* "profit." To become or to make better. To raise to a higher or more desirable quality, value, or condition.

Improvise: To compose and perform or deliver a speech (or music, verse, drama, etc.) without previous thought or preparation. From Latin *in,* "not" and *provire,* "to foresee."

In-house: When the audience is composed only of employees of the same company.

Influence: The power to produce effects on the actions or thoughts of others. From Latin *in,* "in" and *fluere,* "to flow."

Inspire: To have an invigorating influence on someone; to move them to a particular feeling or idea. To breathe life into an idea in their minds. From Latin *in,* "into" and *spirare,* "to breathe."

Instruct: To impart knowledge or skill. To build a new knowledge base within listeners' minds. From Latin *in,* "in" and *struere,* "to build."

Interact: To act on each other. Refers to the audience and/or the presenter communicating with each other in verbal or nonverbal manner.

Interpretation: The presenter or the audience's explanation and/or understanding of the meaning of the ideas under discussion.

Intro: Slang term for an introduction.

Introducer: The person who introduces the speaker and usually leads the audience into a look within the speaker's history. Also see *Announcer, Emcee, Master of Ceremonies, MC,* and *Toastmaster.* From Latin *intro,* "within" and *ducere,* "to lead."

Introduction: A carefully written opener about the speaker used by the introducer at the beginning of your speech. A "halo," with your credits, achievements, and honors, explains why this speaker, on this date, for this audience.

IPA: The International Platform Association. A U.S.-based association for public speakers.

Irony: A sarcastic or humorous way of speaking, where you say the opposite of what you mean, as when "Isn't that sweet?" means "That's hideous." (See *Sarcasm.*)

Juice: Electricity or electric power.

Keynote: Originally, the fundamental point of a speech; today it refers to the main speech at a meeting. One of the featured spots at an event. Usually connected with a prime time at the event, such as a meal function or to open or close an event, to the entire convention in the main room. Often the celebrity speaker. Sets tone of the convention and carries out its theme.

Laugh: 1. Methods of expressing mirth, appreciation of humor and merriment, and so on. 2. Something that causes laughter—for example, a joke, gag, or anecdote. "I get the laugh by doing a pratfall as I enter."

Lavaliere: A hands-free microphone that attaches to your lapel or part of your clothing, as opposed to a stationary or handheld mike. Can be on a cord or cordless. Originally a lavaliere was a pendant, from the French *la vallière,* referring to a round or oval ornament worn on a chain around the neck (named after Louise de la Vallière, 1644–1710, mistress of Louis XIV).

Lectern: A small desk or stand with a sloping top from which you lecture. (See *Lecture.*) Sometimes it has a stationary or handheld mike attached, a shelf underneath, and a light. Sometimes called (many will argue incorrectly) the podium. (See *Podium.*)

Lecture: A discourse given before an audience. The archaic meaning of the word is "the act of reading aloud." From Latin *legere,* "to read."

Lighting: The providing of light or the state of being lighted. Refers to the way a stage or presentation area is illuminated.

Limelight: "1. Public attention or notice. 2. A bright light used to illuminate a performer, stage area, and so on, originally produced by heating lime to incandescence." (*Funk & Wagnalls, Microlibrary 1.1,* © 1990–1992, by Inductell.)

Lingo: The specialized vocabulary and idiom of a profession or class. Dates from the 1600s; an apparent alteration of Latin *lingua,* "tongue."

Malapropism: The absurd misuse of words.

Master: 1. A person eminently skilled in something, such as an occupation, art, or science. 2. Of or pertaining to a master from which copies are made: in photography, a master film (also called a copy negative); in recording, an audio or video tape or disk from which duplicates may be made; in printing, the camera-ready piece used to make other copies for handouts, workbooks, overheads, and so on.

Master of ceremonies: The person who acts as a moderator and connects the separate sessions at a meeting together. Also see *Announcer, Emcee, Introducer, MC,* and *Toastmaster.*

Materials: The things you use in your presentations—for example, handouts, products, giveaways, or workbooks.

MC: Pronounced as it is spelled, it is an abbreviation of *master of ceremonies.* Sometimes spelled emcee. May be used as a noun or verb. Also see *Announcer, Emcee, Introducer, Master of Ceremonies,* and *Toastmaster.*

Media: 1. All the ways of communicating with the public, such as radio and television, newspapers, and magazines. 2. An area or form of artistic expression, or the materials used by the artist or speaker. The media a speaker uses would be the tools he or she uses, such as overheads or videos. Dianna Booher, a business communications expert, says, ". . . or, used more loosely when referring to speakers, 'media' may refer to pantomime, magic, drama, or any other means of conveying a message or feeling other than words." *Media* is the plural form of *medium;* it was first used in reference to newspapers two centuries ago and meant "an intervening agency, means, or instrument."

Meeting planner: The person in charge of all planning for the meeting—logistics, meals, hotel arrangements, room sets, travel, and often hiring of the speakers. Often called just the planner.

Mellifluous: When your words flow sweetly, like honey. From Latin *mel,* "honey" and *fluere,* "to flow."

Mesmerize: To hypnotize. A presenter can so captivate his or her listeners that they seem to be hypnotized. From the 1820s, referring to the infamous Austrian physician Franz or Frieidrich Anton Mesmer, a rather dubious pioneer in hypnosis who lived from 1733 to 1815. "Often accused of being a magician and charlatan, Mesmer treated neurotic patients using iron magnets and hypnosis, which he originated. Hypnosis, or 'mesmerism,' later became an accepted psychotherapeutic technique." (*The New Grolier Multimedia Encyclopedia,* Release 6, © 1993 Grolier, Inc.)

Metaphor: A figure of speech in which one object is likened to another by speaking of it as if it were that other, where a term or phrase is applied to something to which it is not literally applicable in order to suggest a resemblance, as in "A mighty fortress is our God," or "He was a lion in battle." (See *Simile.*) From Greek *meta,* "beyond, over" and *pherein,* "to carry."

Mic: (See *Microphone.*) Slang for microphone. Pronounced MIKE. *Mic* was considered an incorrect abbreviation of *microphone* for many years, but the brand-new dictionaries have finally given in to the influence of the notation on the back of all those tape players (you know, there by the hole where you plug in the microphone that says "mic").

Microphone: An instrument that causes sound waves to be generated or modulated through an electric current, usually for the purpose of transmitting or recording speech or music. There are many types. The most common for presenters are handheld, with or without a cord; stationary, usually attached to a lectern or a mike stand; and lavaliere or hands-free.

Mike: Slang for microphone. (See *Microphone.*)

Mixed metaphor: A mixed metaphor is the use in the same expression of two or more metaphors that are incongruous or illogical when combined, as in "The president will put the ship of state on its feet." "He kept a tight rein on his boiling passions."

Module: A self-contained section of a presentation.

Multimedia: The combined use of several media, as sound and full-motion video in computer applications. A speaker may use overheads, videos, and/or live music in a multimedia presentation.

muse/Muses: With a lowercase m, the genius or powers characteristic of presenters, poets, thinkers, and the like. Since ancient times these artsy sorts have invoked the appropriate Muse for aid when performing and creating. Although the term can refer to any power regarded as inspiring, the original Muses were sister goddesses, originally given as Aoede (song), Melete (meditation), and Mneme (memory), but latterly and more commonly as the nine daughters of Zeus and Mnemosyne who presided over various arts: Calliope (epic poetry), Clio (history), Erato (lyric poetry), Euterpe (music), Melpomene (tragedy), Polyhymnia (religious music), Terpsichore (dance), Thalia (comedy), and Urania (astronomy).

Nonverbal: All things that do not use spoken words to communicate. Teaching with the use of nonverbal methods, incorporates pictures, games, sounds, feeling, touch, and smell.

NSA: The National Speakers Association (of the United States). There is also an association called the National Speakers of Australia.

Off-color: Material that is naughty, indelicate, indecent, or risqué. Also see *Blue humor.*

Off-the-Cuff: This term allegedly comes from the practice of after-dinner speakers making notes for a speech on the cuff of their shirt sleeve at the last minute, as opposed to preparing a speech well beforehand. It originated in America 1930. (from Christine Ammer, *Have A Nice Day—No Problem,* Dutton, © 1992, p. 254) My mother remembers her grandfather spoke of this practice. He said they used to have celluloid cuffs that would wash right off after the talk.

On site: At the place where an event is held. Also refers to an event where meeting planners preview a hotel or venue as a prospective meeting location.

Orator: A person who delivers an oration (a speech); usually thought of as someone of great eloquence. Dates from the 1300s, and comes from the Latin word for speaker.

Overhead projector: A projector of images from transparent piece of film onto a screen.

Over the edge: See *Edge.*

Oxymoron: A figure of speech in which incongruous, seemingly self-contradictory terms are brought together, as in the phrases "cruel kindness," or "to make haste slowly," or "O heavy lightness, serious vanity!" From Greek *oxys,* "sharp" and *moros,* "foolish."

PA: The public address system. The loudspeaker equipment that amplifies sound to the audience.

Panel: A small group of presenters selected to hold a discussion on a particular subject. Audiences are usually encouraged to participate in a question-and-answer period.

Pantomime: The art or technique of conveying emotions, actions, feelings, and so on, by gestures without speech. A style of a play and a type acting. From Greek *panto,* "of all" and *mimos,* "imitator."

Passion: Any intense, extreme, or overpowering emotion or feeling. From Latin *pati,* "to suffer."

Patter: 1. Specialized technical phrases and terminology exclusive to an industry. 2. The usually glib and rapid speech or talk used by a humorist/magician while performing. 3. Any standard material used by a presenter that accompanies his or her shtick. 4. Speakers might speak or sing a rapid-fire patter song or speech. 5. When you speak in a staccato fashion, it can be called patter.

Way back when, in the Catholic faith, the priest would speak in Latin. The priests would say the Pater noster (Our Father) in a very fast, mechanical manner, and it came to be known as patter.

Philosophy: 1. The study of the principles of reality in general. 2. The love of wisdom, and the search for it. 3. The general laws that furnish the rational explanation of anything. 4. Practical wisdom; fortitude. From Greek *philosophos,* "lover of wisdom."

Photo-quality: See *Camera-ready.*

Pit: 1. The area of the theatre where the musicians are located. 2. The main floor of the auditorium of a theater, especially the rear part; also, the audience sitting in this section. 3. Great distress or trouble, as when the presenter feels he or she is doing a poor job.

Pithy: Forceful; effective: brief and meaningful in expression; full of vigor, substance, or meaning; succinct, pointed, meaty, concise. A

Middle English term from the 1300s. Pith is the important or essential core or heart of the matter. Its archaic meaning was the spinal cord or bone marrow.

Plagiarism: An act of artistic or literary theft. This word goes back to the Latin word *plagiarus,* meaning "kidnapping"—especially keeping and stealing of the child, not the act of holding it for ransom. So when you plagiarize, you use someone else's words or thoughts as your own you kidnap them.

Planner: See *Meeting planner.*

Plant: A person set up in the audience to help the speaker by asking a prearranged question to warm the audience up or being part of a predesigned act. The plant has rehearsed or prepared his or her reactions and comments to appear spontaneous to the rest of the audience. (See *Shill.*)

Platform: 1. The raised area where speakers stand when they address an audience. Also called the dais, podium, riser, or stage. 2. A public statement of the principles, objectives, and policy of a political party. My theory is that since in the past politicians always stated their policy from the platform, so eventually the statement itself became known as the platform.

Plug: An advertisement not in the form of a formal ad—usually a mention, either given verbally from the platform or written in a publication, to help promote a product or service.

PMT: Acronym for photomechanical transfer. See *Camera-ready.*

Podium: Often a riser or risers; a small stage; also called dais, platform, or riser. This word comes from the same root as *pedal* and *podiatrist,* (the Greek word *podion,* diminutive of *pous, podos,* meaning foot). So the podium is literally the place you step on. However, common usage is wearing away at the correct translation of this word. Although not all new dictionaries have given in to those who insist on calling the lectern a podium, sometimes *podium* will be used to refer to the lectern. Both of the unabridged dictionaries I used here say a podium can be called a lectern, but list it as the third and last definition. However, the abridged Funk & Wagnalls dictionary does not list a lectern as a correct synonym for a podium. So, you can call the lectern a podium if you like, but those of the old school will raise a condescending eyebrow at you.

Polish: To add the final touches of refinement to your presentation to make it complete and perfect. From Latin *polire,* "to smooth."

Pontificate: Today it means to act or speak pompously or dogmatically, with an attitude of "I don't care to be questioned or challenged, I am the expert!" It also means to perform the office of a pontiff. What is a pontiff and why should you care? Well, that's what I asked myself, but knowing does help explain this words history. It refers to the Roman Catholic Church. In ancient Rome, a pontifex was a priest belonging to the pontifical college, the highest priestly ground that had supreme jurisdiction in religious matters. Back then the Church had the final say in all matters, no questions asked—or, at least, appreciated. From Latin *pons, pontis,* "bridge" and *facere,* "to make," it must have originally meant those who helped our understanding by making a bridge for our minds.

PR: Abbreviation of public relations—promotion, publicity, advertising—all the tools of keeping a speaker in the public's eye.

Pratfall: Used in theatre to mean a fake fall. Thought of as U.S. slang, but some trace it back to the 16th century. It means a humiliating fall, often on the buttocks. There is an old English word *praett,* chiefly Scottish, meaning a lowdown trick, and many think this word comes from that. However *prat* is a word from the 1500s meaning buttocks, so perhaps this is where it comes from.

Preoccupation: When the mind is fully engaged and engrossed, energy and attention are fully directed (hopefully at whatever the presenter wants it engrossed by!). From Latin *praeoccupare,* "to seize beforehand."

Press kit: A promotional package that includes the speaker's letters of recommendation, audio and/or visual tapes, bio, articles written by and about the speaker, and other promotional materials. The name originates from promotional packages that were originally sent to the press (newspapers, media, etc.) to help promote someone.

Problem solving: A system of teaching through audience involvement exercises that present a problem to the group and or subgroups for which they attempt to find solutions.

Process: The logical series of steps the listener or presenter must take to complete an exercise or deliver a concept.

Processing: The contemplation of the idea(s) presented; the logical series of thoughts the listeners must send through their minds to arrive at a conclusion.

Product: An items the speaker has available for sale: usually books, audio cassettes, videos, workbooks, posters, and so on.

Production company: A vendor that help produce a meeting or event. A production company might handle the taping, lighting, and sound, and on occasion may even bring in the speakers and entertainers.

Professional speaker: A public speaker who is paid a fee for performances.

Project: To use words or your force of character to send forth a visualized idea or concept into the minds of the listener. From Latin *pro,* "before" and *jacere,* "to throw."

Projection: To use the voice so it can be heard clearly and at a distance. From Latin *pro,* "before" and *jacere,* "to throw."

Projector: An apparatus for sending a picture onto a screen—for example, an overhead projector, slide projector, or film projector.

Promotional package: See *Press kit.*

Prompter: 1. In a theater, one who follows the lines and prompts the actors. 2. An electronic device that displays a magnified written text so that it is visible to the presenter on a clear screen but is invisible to the audience. The trade name, TelePrompTer, is often used to mean the device itself, just as we open call any copy machine a Xerox, regardless of the fact that it was actually manufactured by another company.

Prop: 1. The dictionary definition is any portable object: projector, overheads, notes, flip charts, marker pens, notepad, calendar, slides, multimedia shows, whiteboard, chalkboard, and so on. However, in common usage among professional presenters it gets fuzzy. I did a survey of 75 presenters on this one word trying to get a consensus of what current common usage dictates, and found there is this second, but not universal school of thought: 2. Some presenters make a distinction between "traditional" visual aids or learning aids (overheads, flip charts, etc.) and less traditional paraphernalia (puppets, musical instruments). This group feels that only less traditional paraphernalia qualify as props, and props are three-dimensional items. Jack Mingo (famous for his *Coach Potato* book) says, ". . . if I were feeling literal, technical, grouchy and argumentative, I would refer to chalkboards as part of the 'set;' flipboards, slides, chalk and pointers as part of the 'visual aids' (the tools that make the presentation possible); and the stuffed animals, puppets, birds' nests, and other cool stuff as 'props.' "

   Although "prop" has come to mean anything that "props up" (supports) a presentation, that is a later double entendre; the term actually comes from the theatrical slang for "stage property."

Psychobabble: Using words from psychiatry or psychotherapy that are ponderous and often not entirely accurate; popularized by a book of the same title (1977) by U.S. journalist Richard D. Rosen.

Public domain: Material and things for which the copyright or patent has expired or that never had any such protection. This is material anyone can use and not credit.

Public seminar: Seminar that is open to the public. Tickets are sold to individuals.

Public service bureau: See *Community service speakers' bureau.*

Public speaker: Someone who speaks in public.

Pulpit: An elevated stand or desk for a preacher in a church. From the Latin *pulpitum,* "scaffold, stage."

Punch line: The line or word that delivers the impact, the fun, the hit of the message.

Q&A: The question and answer session of a presentation.

Rapport: Harmony or sympathy of relation; agreement; accord, fellowship, camaraderie, understanding. From French *rapporter,* to bring back or report.

Rehearse: Today, we prepare for public performance by going over those rough spots until they are smoothed out. From Latin *herce,* "to harrow"—a farm term for going over the ground over and over to break up the rough spots.

Repartee: A quick and witty reply, or a succession of clever retorts to give quick thrust, as in verbal fencing that will slice (divide) the listener in two. Sorry, a bit of a grim analogy there as this word comes from Latin *re,* "again" and *partir,* "to part or divide."

Repeat engagement/repeat booking: When a speaker does a second booking for the same client.

Repertoire: The complete list or supply (or repertory) of dramas an actor or theatre can produce that are prepared and ready to perform. For speakers, the speeches and/or segments/modules the speaker has available. From Latin *reperterium,* "catalog, inventory." (See also *Repertory.*)

Repertory: An ordered list, index, or catalog. See also *Repertoire.*

Resistance: Unwillingness of the audience or the presenter to understand or accept a concept, idea, or experience.

Retort: To cast back a like reply, or hurl back a comment. From Latin *re,* "again" and *torquere,* "to bend or twist." From the same root word as *torture* (interesting!).

Riser: A short, portable platform used to raise an area in the of front of the room so that the presentation may be more easily seen by the audience. A portable stage, dais, or podium. Also called *dais, platform, podium,* or *stage.*

Roast: An event where the guest of honor is criticized and/or ridiculed severely in the name of fun.

Roastee: The guest of "honor" at a roast.

Roaster: Individual participants doing the roasting at a roast.

Roastmaster: The master of ceremonies at a roast.

Role play: An audience participation exercise where the audience and/or presenter pretends to have the attitudes, actions, and dialog of another, usually in a make-believe situation. This sort of exercise is used in an effort to heighten understanding of differing points of view or social interaction.

Rostrum: The dais or stage area used by a speaker. The platform for speakers in the Forum of ancient Rome was decorated with the bows of ships captured in war. Guess what these bows were called? You got it! Rostrums. From this, *rostrum* came to mean any platform for speakers in ancient Rome.

Running gag: A joke, phrase, or fun bit of business that makes reference to others told before.

Sarcasm: A sarcastic remark tends to describe a person's weaknesses, vanities, absurdities, and so on in subtly disparaging terms. Irony is a more limited form of sarcasm. From Greek *sarkazein*, "to tear flesh (*sarx*) and gnash teeth." (See also *Irony*).

Saver: Anything used to salvage a part of the presentation that seems to need rescuing.

Seasoning the presentation: Things that increase the enjoyment, zest, and/or impact of a presentation.

Seasoning the presenter: The act or aging process by which the presenter, just like lumber, is rendered fit for use. All the experiences that make the presenter a better communicator and performer.

Segue: Pronounced SEG-way. The words or ways you transition from one topic to another in conversation or a speech. Ideally, segues should be logical or seamless. For example, if you open your talk on leadership with, "My, the weather is terrible today. And speaking of weather, great leaders need to use their skills in all weather—good and bad. So turn with me to page one of your handout," the transition from weather to leaders is a segue. The second transition, from weather to handouts, is a merely a change of thought.

Segue was originally a term in music, meaning to proceed without pause from one sound or theme to another.

Seminar: Classroom-type lecture. Seminars can last from one hour to many days. Usually an educational session. At a convention, the breakout or concurrent sessions are often referred to as seminars. A seminar is usually thought of as having more lecture formats than a workshop.

Sharing with the audience: Refers to the inclusion of the audience in the magic and ambience the presenter tries to create. Also refers to those times the presenter or an audience member shares some of the his or her (usually personal) self, thoughts, or feelings, possibly with some self-disclosure.

Shill: A plant in the audience (see *Plant*), but *shill* can have a negative connotation of a connection with a hustle. Perhaps a person who poses as a bystander and decoy to encourage an audience to bet, buy, or bid. This word seems to date from the 1920s.

Shtick/shtik: From the Yiddish word *stück*, meaning a bit, part, or piece. In about the 1960s in the U.S. it came to mean a performer's special piece of business, an attention-getting device.

Sight gag: A comic effect produced by visual means rather than by spoken lines, as a pie in the face or pratfall. The term came into the use in the mid-1940s.

Sight line: Any of the lines of sight between the audience and the stage/presentation area. When a presenters is off stage, he or she is out of the sight line, in a place where the audience can't see the speaker.

Signature story: A story credited to a specific person that is as unique as that person's signature. These sorts of stories are not in the public domain. It is considered very bad form to use someone else's signature story, especially without crediting the owner.

Simile: A figure of speech in which two unlike things are explicitly compared, as in, "She is like a rose." Similes use words such as *like, as,* and *so,* as opposed to metaphors, which simply place the two items to be compared side by side. (See *Metaphor.*) "Simile is a literary device to conjure up a vivid picture; 'an Alpine peak like a frosted cake' is a simile. A metaphor omits "like" or "as", the words of comparison; 'the silver pepper of the stars' is a metaphor. A comparison brings together things of the same kind or class." (*Funk & Wagnalls, Microlibrary 1.1,* © 1990–1992, by Inductell.)

Site: The location of the meeting, sometimes called the venue. (See also *Venue.*)

Slander: Oral utterance tending to damage another's reputation, means of livelihood, and so on. From Latin *scandalum,* "cause of stumbling."

Slick: See *Camera-ready.*

Slide: 1. In the U.S., most often this will mean 35-mm slides. 2. In English-speaking countries other than the U.S., *slide* tends to mean an overhead slide transparency. 3. Slang for avoiding an issue.

Sound/sound system: The audio sound amplification system for speakers.

Sound booth: The area were the controls for the sound are kept; referred to as a booth regardless of how it is set up. Often it will be located on a dais in a corner of the room and will be combined with the tech booth. May also be referred to as the A/V booth or A/V area (See also *Tech booth.*)

Speakers' bureau: A booking or sales company that provides speakers and humorists for meeting planners. They usually represent speakers on a nonexclusive basis.

Special events company: A company that brings in all kinds of special effects and theatrical acts (and occasionally the presenters) to an event.

Spokesperson, spokesman/woman: A person who speaks for or in the name of and/or in behalf of another person or a company or association.

Stage fright: Fear and panic that sometimes attacks presenters.

Stage left: The side of the stage that is left of center as the presenter faces the audience. Also called *left stage.*

Stage lights: The lights that illuminate the stage area.

Stage right: The side of the stage that is right of center as the presenter faces the audience. Also called *right stage.*

Stage: 1. Any place a speech, play, or production is given. Also called *dais, platform, podium,* or *riser.* 2. To plan and organize the presentation for its best dramatic effect.

Stammer: To speak or utter haltingly, with involuntary repetitions or prolonged sounds, or with irregular repetitions of syllables or sounds. May be a temporary condition caused by stage fright or another emotion, or a psychophysical condition requiring professional treatment. From German *stammern.*

Stock in trade: For presenters, the stock used in the craft of speaking— possibly stories, statistics, tapes, video, props, and so on. In the 1600s it came into usage to mean the goods kept on sale by a dealer, shopkeeper, or peddler. Also referred to as stock of trade. Also means the equipment used in conducting a trade or business. By the 1770s it also came to mean what you kept on hand in your mental facility. (*Oxford English Dictionary,* vol. 16, second edition, Clarindon Press, Oxford, 1989, p. 742–743)

Swan song: A farewell appearance, an artist's last work. Based on a the myth developed by the ancient Greek that stated that swans are mute but burst into song just before they die.

Symposium: Today this means a meeting for discussion of a particular subject, or a collection of comments or opinions brought together; perhaps a series of brief essays or articles on the same subject, as in a magazine. From *symposion,* which basically meant a Greek drinking party.

Tailoring: The speaker's adjustment of the material to the particular needs of the audience.

Talent: 1. A special natural ability or aptitude. 2. The speaker or performer. In the gospel of Matthew, Chapter 25, is the story of the master who gave money to each of his three servants. In those times a talent was an archaic unit of measure for money. When the master returned, two of the servants had invested the money he had left with them, so it had grown. But the third had just buried it in the ground. The first two servants were praised and given more to work with. The third servant not only did not have his talents increased, his master was so angry with him that he took the talent away from him and sent the servant out into sorrow. Today we call our special abilities talents because of this story, the moral being "Use it or lose it!"

Tantalize: To tease or torment by repeated frustration of hopes or desires. Derived from the myth of Tantalus, a son of Zeus, sent to Hades. His punishment was to sit in a big pool, very thirsty, but when he tried to drink, the water pulled back. The fruit trees at the edge would pull their fruit back if he tried to reach them—tantalizing poor Tantalus.

Theatre-style seating: When the seating for the audience is set up in rows, much as in a theatre, with no tables.

Tech booth: The area of the meeting from which the sound, lights, and technical equipment are controlled. Referred to as a booth regardless of how it is set up. Often it will be located on a dais in a corner of the room. The sound booth is often part of the tech booth. (See *Sound booth.*)

Tech crew: The people who operate the sound, lights, and technical equipment.

Technobabble: Using words from technology that are ponderous and often not entirely accurate. (See *Psychobabble.*)

TelePrompTer: See *Prompter.*

Testimonial: Usually a written letter of recommendation from a former buyer or colleague who is familiar with your work.

Theme: The moving thread that weaves throughout the presentation.

Toast: The act of drinking to someone's health or to some sentiment and the person named in the sentiment. How the custom began is unknown, but raising a glass in a toast is steeped in our antiquity. Ulysses drank to Achilles' health in the *Odyssey;* Atilla drinks to the health of everyone in *The Rise and Fall of the Roman Empire.* But in the Shakespearean era it seems the custom of having a spiced piece of toast in a drink to flavor it came along. Perhaps the custom of toasting to your health comes from the notion that the person being honored also added flavor by their existence. From Latin *torrere,* "to parch."

Toastmaster/mistress: A person who, at public dinners, announces the toasts, calls upon the various speakers, and so on. Also see *Announcer, Emcee, Introducer, Master of Ceremonies,* and *MC.*

Toastmasters International: One of the largest personal development associations in the world to assist in building confidence in public communication skills.

Tongue in cheek: Sentiment spoken with irony or humor. "It first appeared in print in a book published in 1845 called *The Ingolds by Legends,* in which the author, Richard Barham, reports a Frenchman as saying, 'Superbe! Magnifique!' (with his tongue in his cheek)." (from William Morris, *Morris Dictionary of Word and Phrase Origins,* second edition, Harper & Row, 1988)

Track: The type of communication you use at any given time to teach—for instance, video, audio, lecture, audience participation, and so on. The expression comes from the recording industry, where it refers to a discrete, separate recording that is combined with other parts of a musical recording to produce the final aural version.

Trainer: One who conducts workshops and training sessions. Participants are given assignments, break into small groups, then come back together.

Transcribe: To copy or recopy in handwriting, typewriting, or electrical recording a presentation or program of any type. From Latin *trans,* "over" and *scribere,* "to write."

Triad: A discussion group of three people.

Two-step seminar: A free seminar where attendees are encouraged to buy a second seminar or set of products.

Understand: To come to know the meaning or import of, to have comprehension or mastery of. From Anglo-Saxon *understandan,* "to stand under or among"; hence, to comprehend. (I wonder if this is where we get the expression "over their heads.")

Up my/your/his sleeve: A backup strategy, idea, or other item that will serve you in a time of need. From an audience perception of a magician who makes things happen suddenly and magically. The assumption is that the only way the magician could achieve that magical result is have something up his sleeve.

Upstage: 1. The part of the stage farthest away from the audience. (see *Downstage*). 2. To overshadow another presenter or performer by moving upstage and forcing the performer to turn away from the audience. 4. When you steal the focus of the audience in any way.

From these theater usages it has also come to mean when you outdo another professionally or socially. In ancient times, theatres were often located in a small ravine. The audience was on one hillside, the stage on the other. Downstage was the point that was the farthest down the hill. Upstage was the point farthest up the hill.

Velox: A brand name for a film paper. See *Camera ready.*

Venue: 1. Site of a meeting or event; often a hotel, conference center, convention center, college, or restaurant. 2. The position, side, or ground taken by the presenter in an presentation, argument, or debate. Originally used to mean the place where the action was. Middle English used *venue* to mean an attack, probably because it came from the Latin *venire,* "to come." No doubt the battle cry of, "They're coming! They're coming!" could easily eventually come to mean attack.

Vignette: Pronounced VIN-yet. A description or short literary work that depicts a story subtly and delicately. In the mid 1700s the title page of a book or at the beginning or end of a chapter would often have a decorative design or small illustration with lovely, delicate vines running through it. The French called these vignettes, from the word *vigne*, "vine."

Vitae: See *Biographical sketch, Curriculum vitae.*

Wings: Sides of stage in an auditorium, out of sight of audience.

Wireless: A wireless mike without a cord. Works by radio waves through the PA system.

Workshop: Educational, classroom-type session, usually with handouts or workbooks. Rarely lasts less than one hour, could be as long as many days. Usually considered to involve more audience participation and experiential exercises and project assignments than a seminar.

Index

Add-on events, 7–8
Adventure-related opportunities, 19
Advertising. *See also* Publicity
  as prospect source, 26, 121
  targeted, 15, 67–68
Affiliate programs, 127
Agents, booking through, 32–41
Air conditioning, 160
Alcohol, 160
Allen, Steve, 110
Alliances. *See* Teaming
Amazon.com, 112, 124–125, 127, 142
American Business Women's Association (ABWA), 77
American Red Cross, 149
American Society of Association Executives (ASAE), 27, 66, 77
American Society of Training and Development (ASTD), 77
Apprenticeships 7, 103
Art of War, The (Sun Tzu), 7
Assistants, presentation, 152, 156–159, 163
Associated Press, 88
Associations:
  joining, 76–78
  marketing to, 25–26
Auction sales, online, 125
Audio tapes. *See* Demo tapes

Authoring, as income generator. *See* Writing
Autographed material, 126
Awards, as publicity tool, 89

Back-of-room sales, 122–124
BarnesandNoble.com, 124
Bartering:
  for ad space, 67–68
  fee-related, 79–83, 118
Birthday cards, as marketing tool, 59, 74
Bomb threats. *See* Safety issues
Bookings, follow-up, 68–73
Books:
  as passive marketing, 2, 63
  publishing issues, 112–113
Bookstores, as clients, 22
Bounceback offers, 121
Branding, 48–49
Breakout sessions, 4
Breaks, midpresentation, 151
Bureaus, speakers'. *See* Speaker's bureaus
Business cards:
  collecting, 69, 126
  as marketing tool, 35, 79, 127, 136
Business cycles, downtime, 144–145

Buyers:
 finding, 25–29
 large companies, 29–32
 likes and dislikes of, 32
 middlemen, 32–41

Calendars, 15, 63, 98
Call waiting, 102
Careerbuilders.com, 10
Catalogs, product, 121, 124–125,
 127
Catering issues, 151–152, 155–156,
 160, 162
Celebrity status, cultivating, 59,
 84–95
Cell phones, emergency use of, 148,
 156, 165, 166
Census. *See* U.S. census
Chambers of commerce, 17, 23, 25,
 76
Children's programs. *See* Youth pro-
 grams
Churches, as clients, 17
Coaching:
 to improve delivery, 44
 as income stream, 10–11
Cold calling, 30, 83
Collaborating. *See* Teaming
Colleges, as clients, 18
Commercials, 3
Community groups, 17–19, 23–24
Companies, marketing to, 12–14,
 29–31
Computer equipment, 100–102
Conference calls:
 as time savers, 107
 as value-added service, 11
Consortiums. *See* Teaming
Consultants, 9–10
Continuing education units (CEUs),
 19–20
Contracts, 43, 81–82, 150
Cooperative marketing, 52. *See also*
 Teaming
Copyrighting issues, 93, 116–117

Corporations, 12–14, 29–30
Cover letters, 136
Credit cards, as sales incentive, 124
Cruise-related opportunities, 19
Customization, 50, 54–55, 116–119

Demo tapes, 111–112, 138–140,
 153
Desktop conferencing, 21
Direct mail advertising, 15, 66
Directories:
 categories of, 85–86
 listing yourself in, 66–67
 marketing, 28
Disraeli, Benjamin, 48
Distance learning, 12, 20–21
Distributorships, 57
Do's and don'ts:
 bureau-related, 32–41
 client-related, 32, 83
 speech-related, 46–47
 for suspicious packages,
  163–166
Downtime, 144–145
Dressing professionally, 129, 151
Dun & Bradstreet, 17

eBay, 125, 129
Economic Development Centers, as
 clients, 18
Economic down cycles, 144–145
Education:
 continuing, 19–20
 distance learning, 20–21
 virtual seminars, 20
 80/20 rule, 42
E-mail:
 as part of messaging center, 101
 as passive marketing, 53
 as publicity generator, 15, 142
Emcees. *See* Masters of ceremonies
 (MCs)
Emergency situations, 147–150,
 156–158, 161, 163–166

Employees. *See* Office staffing
Endorsements. *See* Testimonials
Entertainment coordinators, 7
Evaluation forms, 162. *See also* Rating
    sheets
Exhibits. *See* Trade shows
Expert witnesses, 3
E-zines:
    for information gathering, 48
    as marketing tool, 15, 116, 121,
        141
    writing for, 51

Facilitators/moderators. *See* Modera-
    tors/facilitators
Family issues, 82, 104, 105–106
Fax systems, 101
Feedback. *See* Rating sheets
Fees and commissions:
    bureau-related, 38–41
    customization-related, 118–119
    menu of services, 2, 14, 52
    negotiating, 79–82
Financial issues. *See also* Fees and
    commissions
    cash reserves, 57, 144
    retirement, 145
Franchises. *See* Distributorships
Franklin, Benjamin, 50
Fred Pryor/CareerTrack, 17
Free speeches. *See* No-fee presenta-
    tions
Fund-raising, 17–18

Gale Database of Publications
    (online), 85
*Gale Directory of Print and Broadcast
    Media,* 85
"Game show" hosts, 5–6
Gifts. *See also* Giveaways
    as promotional strategy, 60–61
    for referrers, 73
Giveaways:
    as attendance reward, 122

Giveaways (*Cont.*):
    versus bribes, 60–61
    as passive marketing, 52, 65
Google search engine:
    for catalogs, 124
    for consulting, 10
    for e-zines, 93–94
    for newswires, 85
Grand Master Hyperlink List of Speak-
    ers' Bureaus (Lilly Walters), 28
Greeting cards, as marketing tool, 59,
    73–74
Guest, Edgar A., 47

Handouts, 52, 116–118, 150
History-related income opportunities,
    7
Hometown markets. *See* Local markets
Hospitality and Sales Marketing Asso-
    ciation (HSMAI), 77
Hospitals, as clients, 17
Hotel staff, 107–108, 151–152,
    155–156
Hotline services, 12

Income opportunities:
    from add-on events, 7–8
    from breakout sessions, 4
    from coaching, 10–11
    as commercial speakers, 3
    from conference calls, 11
    as consultants, 9–10
    customization, 54–55
    distributorships, 57
    as entertainment coordinators, 7
    as executive trainers, 10
    as expert witnesses, 3
    as "game show" hosts, 5–6
    hometown, 55–56
    and hotline services, 12
    as infomercial hosts, 3
    as keynote speakers, 3–4
    as masters of ceremonies, 4–5
    as moderators/facilitators, 5, 9

Income opportunities (*Cont.*):
  from no-fee presentations, 21–24
  overview, 1–2
  as panel facilitators, 5
  from pre and post program events, 7
  from product sales, 109–127
  on the road, 99–102
  from seminars, 3, 8–9, 14–21
  as spokespeople, 13
  from sponsors, 12–13
  from spouse programs, 6
  as trainers, 8
  as tutors, 12
  from video programs, 12
  from writing, 2, 112–113,
    115–116
  from youth programs, 6
Infomercials, 3, 121, 146
Insurance Conference Planners Association, 77
International business, 126, 150
International Group of Agencies and
  Bureaus, 27
Internet. *See also* Web sites
  as classroom, 20–21
  as marketing tool, 121, 124–125,
    127, 141–143
  as publicist, 15
  as resource, 10, 23, 25, 66
Internships, 104
Introducers, 5, 159
Introductions, written, 71

Jaycees, 24
Just-in-Time programs, 8, 20–21

Keynote speakers, 3–4
Kiam, Victor, 106
Kipling, Rudyard, 91
Kiwanis clubs, 18, 24

Lateral marketing, 26, 50–51
Learning Annex, 18
Letterhead, 136

Letters of recommendation, 24. *See
  also* Testimonials
Libraries, as resource, 26, 85, 154
Licensing fees, 119
Lilly Walters' Grand Master Hyper-
  link List of Speakers' Bureaus, 28
Lions clubs, 18, 24
Local markets, 7, 55–56
Lombardi, Vince, Sr., 46

Mackay, Harvey, 90
Magazines, writing for, 92–94
Mailing lists, 16
Maps, 152
Marketing. *See also* Rainmaking
  agents, 32–41
  to associations, 25–26
  to decision makers, 25, 28–30
  directories, 28
  to large companies, 29–32
  promotional materials, 132–143
  referrals, 30–31
  showcasing, 26–28
Marketing plan, 43
Mastermind groups, 11, 44
Masters of ceremonies (MCs), 4–5
Media:
  cultivating, 84–95, 153
  as partner, 18
  as publicist, 15
Meeting Professionals International
  (MPI), 27, 66, 76
Mentors, 44–45
Menu of services, 2, 14, 52
Microsoft Word, 100, 111
Middlemen, as booking agents, 32–41
Moderators/facilitators, 5, 9
Money management. *See* Fees and
  commissions; Financial issues
Monster.com, 10
Murphy's Law, 153

National Association of Campus
  Activities (NACA), 27
National Seminars, 17

National Speakers Association (NSA), 77

Negotiating skills, 78–84

Networking:
  in breakout sessions, 4
  for referrals, 74–75
  showcasing and, 27
  via picture taking, 8

Newsgroups, 121, 142

Newsletters:
  as products, 115–116
  promotional, 15, 51–54, 63–64

Newspapers, as clients, 18

News releases, 87–94

Newswire services, 85, 88

Niche marketing, 49–50

No-fee presentations:
  benefiting from, 21–24
  and expert-witness leads, 3
  and nonprofits, 145
  and showcasing, 27–28

Nordstrom (retail stores), 14

Novak, Kim, 90

Office equipment, 99–102

Office staffing, 102–105

One Hand Typing and Keyboarding Manual (Lilly Walters), 113

One-on-one coaching, 10, 55

One-on-one marketing, 59–62

One-sheets, 136–137

Online auction houses, 125

Panel facilitators, 5

Paperwork, 43–44

Partnerships. *See* Teaming

Passive income, 119–127, 145

Passive marketing, 51–54

PCMA, 66

PDF files, 100–101, 134, 149

Phone seminars, 16

Photos, as marketing tool, 8, 135–136

Postcards, customized, 136

Poynter, Dan, 113

Practice venues, 45

Pre and post program events, 7

Presentation folders, 137–138

Presentations. *See also* Seminars; Speeches
  after the meeting, 162–163
  before the meeting, 155–161
  during the meeting, 161–162
  preparations for, 147–155
  safety issues, 163–166

Press exposure, 87–95

Price/Costco, 14

Problem-solving sessions, 9

Products:
  creating, 109–119
  promoting, 12–14, 16, 51–54
  selling, 16, 119–127

Professional organizations, continuing education, 19–20

Promotional materials:
  business cards, 79, 136
  customized, 50, 135
  demo tapes, 138–140
  one-sheets, 136–137
  preparing, 132–136
  presentation folders, 137–138
  testimonials, 140
  Web sites, 141–143

Promotional strategies:
  advertising, 67–68
  direct mail, 66
  directories, 66–67
  one-on-one marketing, 59–62
  personal aura, 58–59, 68, 129
  tools to enhance, 62–65

PTAs, as clients, 17

Publicity, 15, 86–95, 153–154

Publicity releases, 90–92

Public seminars. *See* Seminars

Publishing issues. *See* Books

Questionnaires, 44. *See also* Surveys

Radio:
  as client, 18

Radio (*Cont.*):
  directories, 66–67
  as marketing tool, 66, 94–95
Radio Shack, 127
Rainmaking:
  basics, 47–58
  getting started, 42–47
  media strategies, 84–95
  networking, 68–84
  promotional strategies, 58–68
  travel-related issues, 95–108
Rating sheets, 71–72, 131, 140, 162
Referrals, 30–31, 68–78
Repeat business, 68–71, 75–76
Resort-related opportunities, 19
Retailers, as clients, 14
Retirement issues, 145–146
Rewards, finders' fees, 73
Rivers, Joan, 22
Roman, George, 88
Rotary clubs, 18, 23, 24, 25
Royalties, 111–112, 145, 153
Ryan, Jack, 130

Safety issues, 147–150, 156–158, 161, 163–166
Salesman's Guide, 28
Sales skills, 78–84
School groups, 17–18, 145
Schools, as clients, 17
Sears, 14
Seating charts, 151
Secretarial services, 103
Secrets of Successful Speakers (Lilly Walters), 130
Self-Publishing Manual, The (Poynter), 113
Seminars:
  in-house, 8–9
  public, 3, 14–21, 31
  selling products at, 122–124
September 11 disaster, 147
Service clubs, 18, 23, 24, 25
Share-the-gate events, 17–19
Shopping channels, 121

Showcasing, 26–28, 80
Slide shows, 8, 9
Smoking, 160
Society of Human Resource Management (SHRM), 77
Software, office, 100–102, 110
Speak and Grow Rich (Lilly and Dottie Walters), 62
"Speaker Expense Dilemma, The" (Lilly Walters), 65
Speakers' bureaus, 32–41
  directories of, 28
  and passive marketing, 54
  and showcasing, 26–27
Speaking industry:
  future of, 146–147
  leadership qualities, 147–154
  profiting from, ix–xi
Speaking Industry Reports (Lilly Walters), x, 1
Speeches:
  expert knowledge, 47–50
  improving, 45–47
  as marketing tool, 68, 128–129
  material for, 110–111, 129–132
  selling products at, 122–124
Spokespeople, corporate, 13
Sponsors, as income source, 12–13
Spouse programs, 6, 55
Staples (retail stores), 14
Sun Tzu, 7
Superpages.com, 23
Support teams, 145
Surveys. *See also* Questionnaires
  of attendees, 54, 154
  by author, x
  marketplace, 130
  as press releases, 88
  rating sheets, 71–72, 131, 140
Swim With the Sharks Without Being Eaten Alive (Mackay), 90

Tapes, demo. *See* Demo tapes
Teaming (sharing resources), 31, 64, 78

Telecoaching, 1, 146
Teleconferencing, 21
Telephones:
    emergency use of, 148, 156, 165, 166
    office systems, 99–100, 101–102
Television, as marketing tool, 66–67
Temp workers, 103
Testimonials, 140
Thank-you notes:
    bureau-related, 40
    presentation-related, 62, 143, 159,
        163
    as promotional strategy, 60, 136
    for referrals, 58, 74
Time savers, 107–108
Toastmasters, 45, 77, 129
Tools of the trade, 99–102, 127–143
Tours, as income generator, 7
Tracking leads, 62–63
Trade journals, 30, 92–94
Trade shows, 68, 125–126, 131
Trainers, 8
Training materials, 110
Travel issues:
    arrival plans, 152
    delays, 154–155
    family-related, 105–106
    minimizing, 145
    packing hints, 151
    scheduling challenges, 96–99,
        106–108
    virtual offices, 95–96, 99–105
Tutors, 12
TV stations:
    as clients, 18
    directories, 66–67

UPI, 88
U.S. census, as source material, 88

Videoconferencing, 21
Video programs. *See also* Demo
    tapes
    as entertainment, 8
    for training, 12
Video tapes. *See* Demo tapes
Virtual seminars, 20–21
Voice mail, 101–102

Walters, Dottie, 90
Walters International Speakers
    Bureau, 65
Web sites. *See also* Internet
    best-seller lists, 132
    career-related, 10
    catalog-related, 124–125
    hot topics, 131
    keynote speakers, 28
    publishing-related, 112
    service clubs, 23
    U.S. census statistics, 88
Williams, Robin, 22
Williamson, Ramon, 1–2
Workbooks, 13, 116–118, 150
Workshops, in-house, 8–9
World Trade Center disaster, 147
Writing:
    books, 2, 63, 112–113
    as income source, 2, 115
    Internet articles, 142
    journal articles, 92–94
    as marketing strategy, 26, 30,
        51–53
    media material, 86–90
    publicity releases, 90–92

Yahoo!, 23, 152
Youth programs, 6, 13, 17–18

About the Author

Lilly Walters is the bestselling author of *What to Say When You're Dying on the Platform* and *Secrets of Superstar Speakers*. She is also a professional speaker, consultant to speakers, and booking agent for speakers.